High Shelf

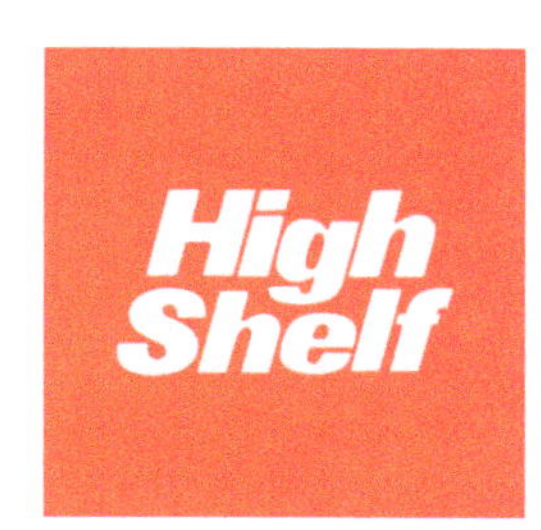

High Shelf XXX. May 2021.

Portland, Oregon.

Paperback ISBN: 978-1-952869-30-3

Cover Image by Andrée-Anne Guay
Design and Layout by C. M. Tollefson
Editing by David Seung & C. M. Tollefson

With special thanks to:
Eric Hoskins, Megan Kim, & River Elizabeth Hall.

High Shelf XXX

May 2021

“Every night I have the same dream,
my teeth are falling into the monster’s lap.
One night I lost all of my teeth.
I could not speak.
I could not scream.
The monster feels sorry for me... ”

Khaled K.E.M.

"Made inarticulate
by snowfall,
the wood surrounds us in silence.

Your small hand,
balled in my own, discerns
my pulse..."

Joe Pagano Jr.

Table Of Contents

Diagnosis

Kimberly Kralowec

You stood there, pre-dreamed—
as sentient weather mulled over
its next offensive. The sun selected
a new, more daring exit from the sky.
In the darkness that followed:
every surface unreflective, brown
silence unrooted, eyes drawn
to the nearest horizons—the rims
of my lenses. Somehow I knew all
the trees had left the city,
and your face had transformed
from male—to musk—your floral
all that was left to sense. If I love
you, that means you'll survive.

The Living Will

J. Heimberger

Give me to the Maple trees.
Send my blood nitrogen-rich
up searching roots to the sapwood.
Pour me amber over strawberry
hearts and Mama's french toast.

Give me to the live oaks
where I might hang in curtains
of Spanish moss and taste rain.
Let me feed the furrowed bark
and heal its lightning scars.

Give my guts to the grasses
where sheep are grazing, thank them,
for the wool that covers my toes
and the strings that fill a room
with strums of hallelujahs.

Give my body to the earthworms
and their five hearts, my ginger hair
to the bird nests for softer landings.
Burn my heart and send it to the stars
in vapor to be breathed again and again.

Sit by the fire and bang on my skull.
Dance your skeletons halfway to dust,
to the drum of bone and the pop of pine,
to this oldest music, freely given,
to this flash of incandescent carbon,
rising into the December blackness.

On Suicide

Hayley Stoddard

Once you slip into those dark waters,
you'll always carry a certain chill with you

like a cold silver key on a chain around your neck,
the choice to walk away, to go swimming

so the aching, the hurting, would be over.
You brush it off again and again, like a fly

hovering above a slice of wet
watermelon on a hot summer day.

FABULA

Mane Hovhannisyan

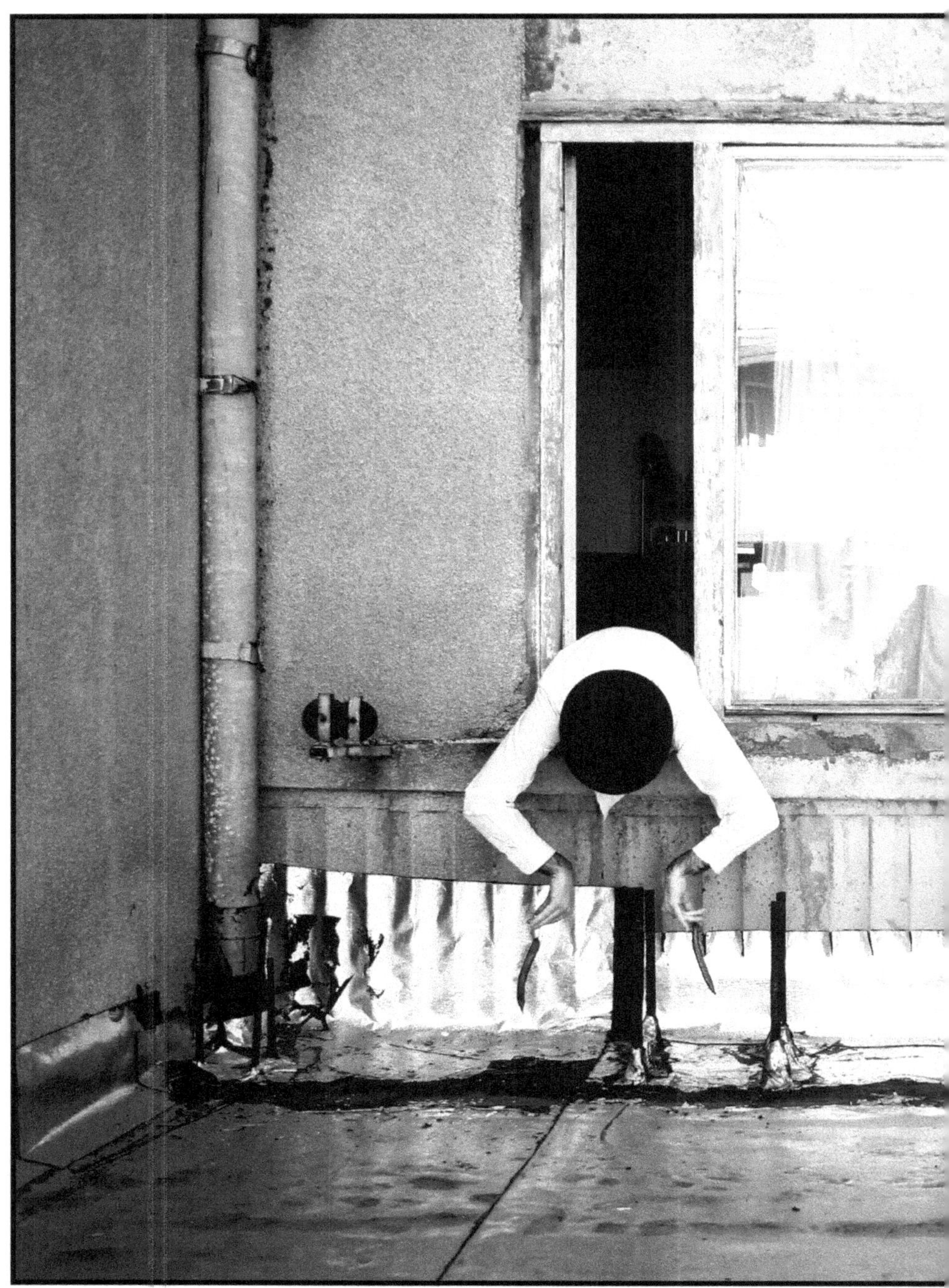

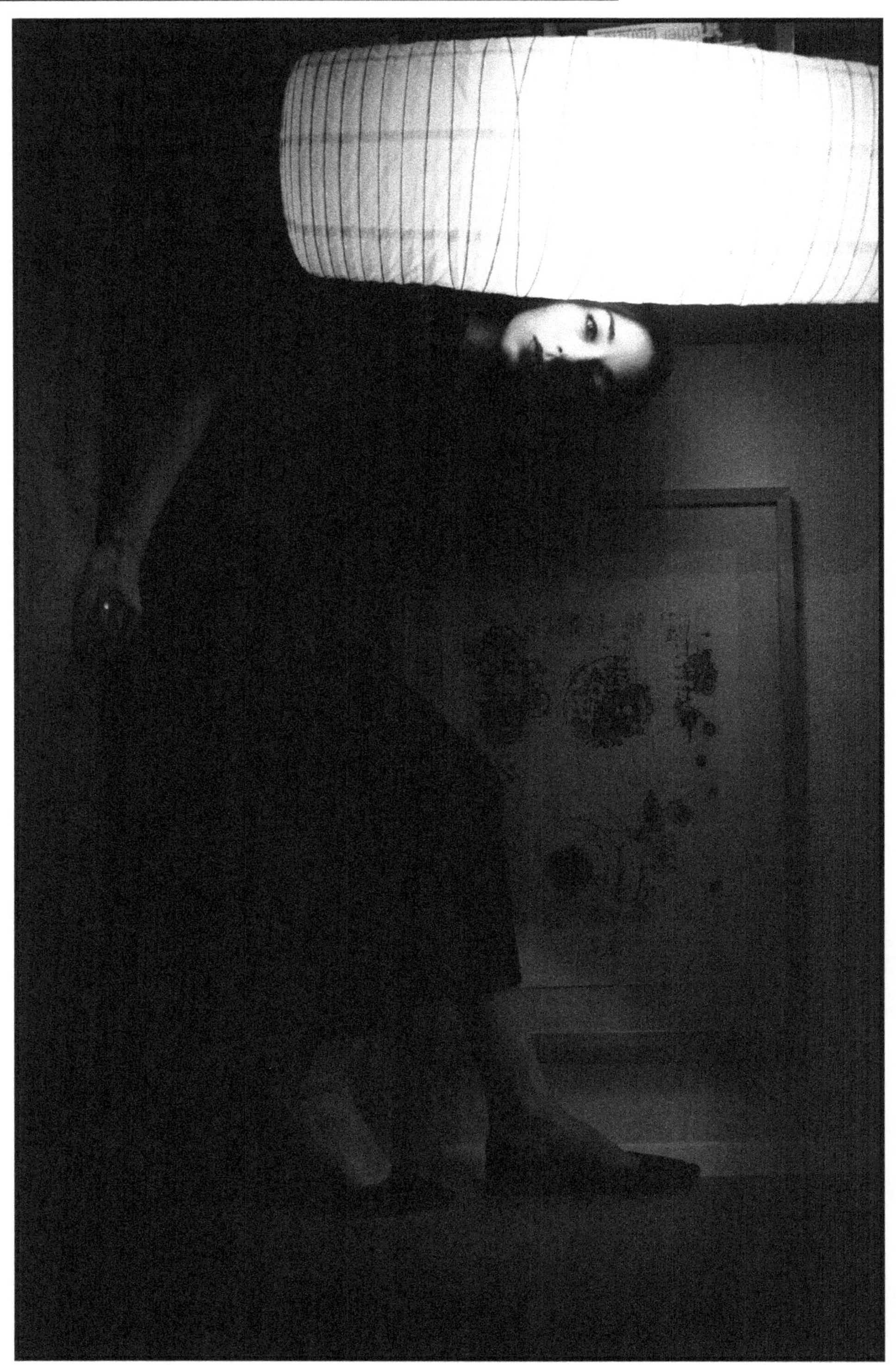

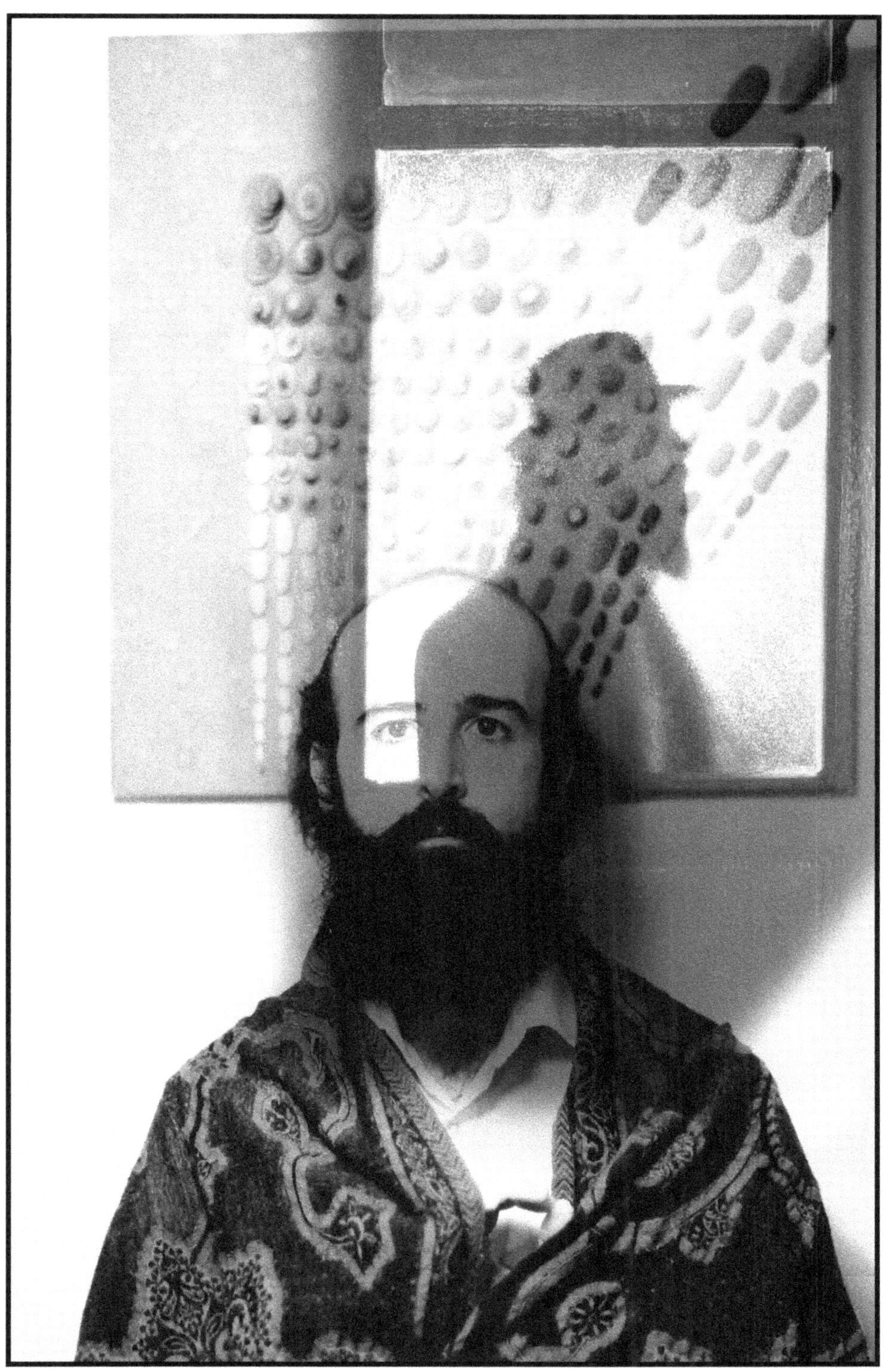

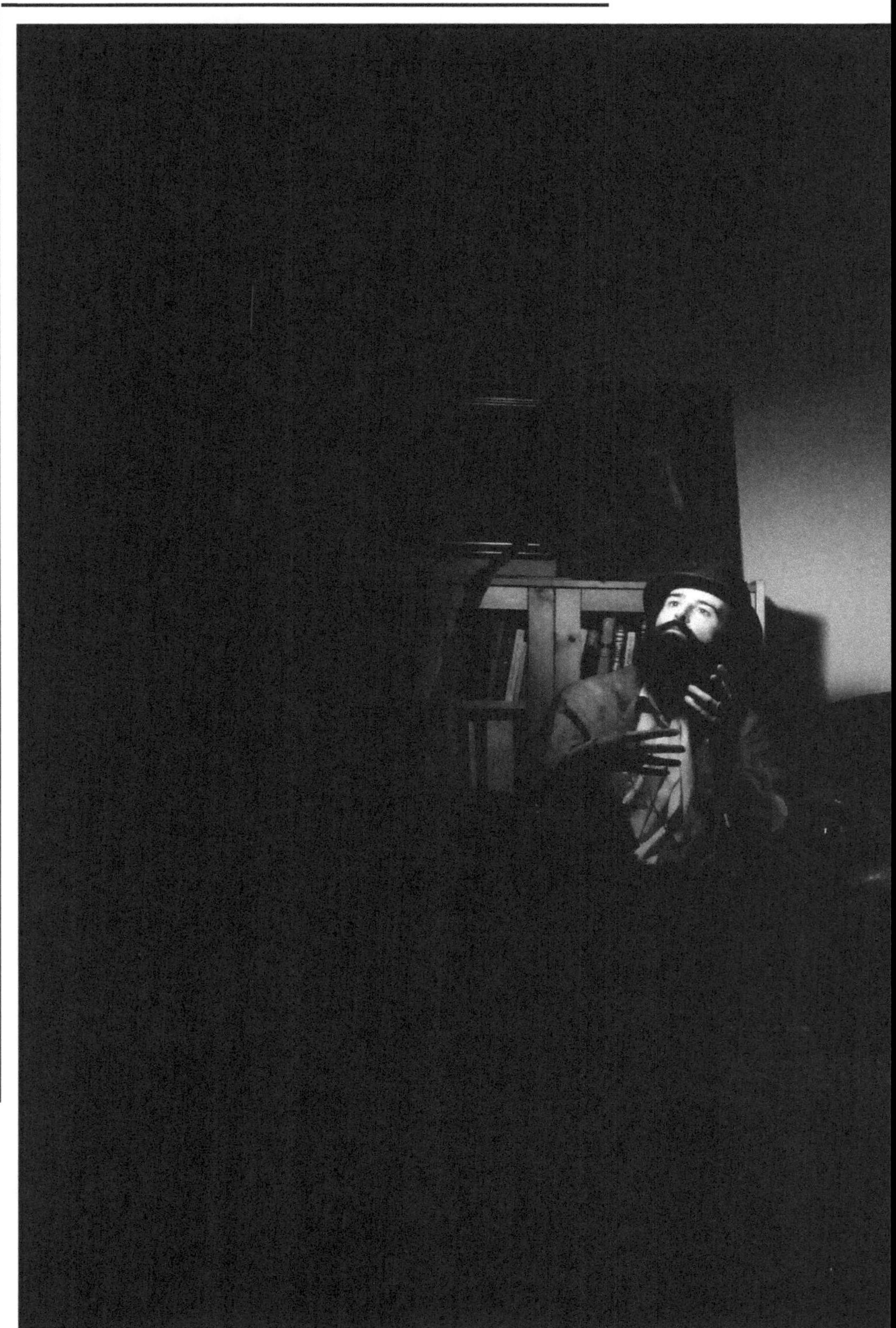

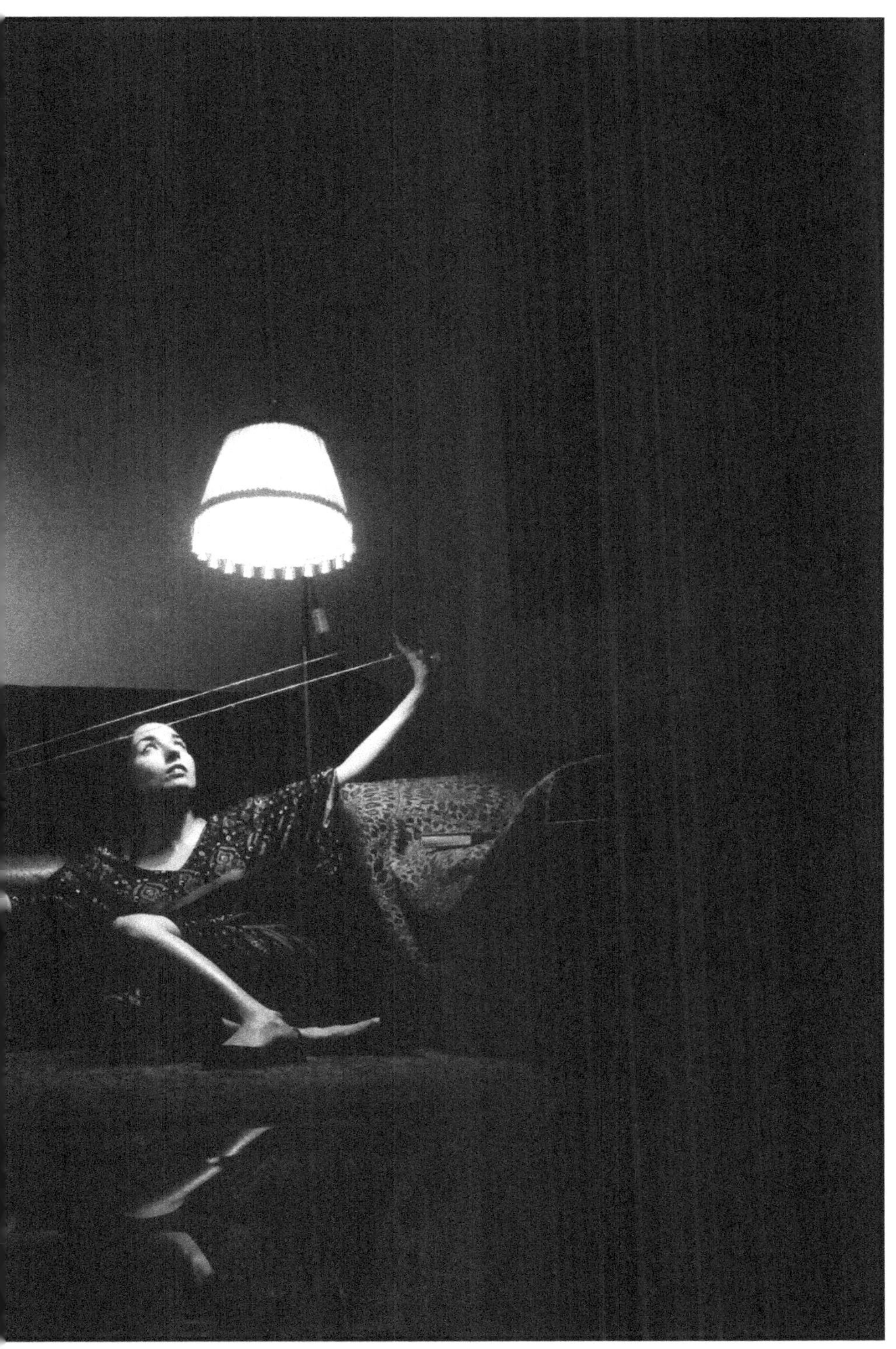

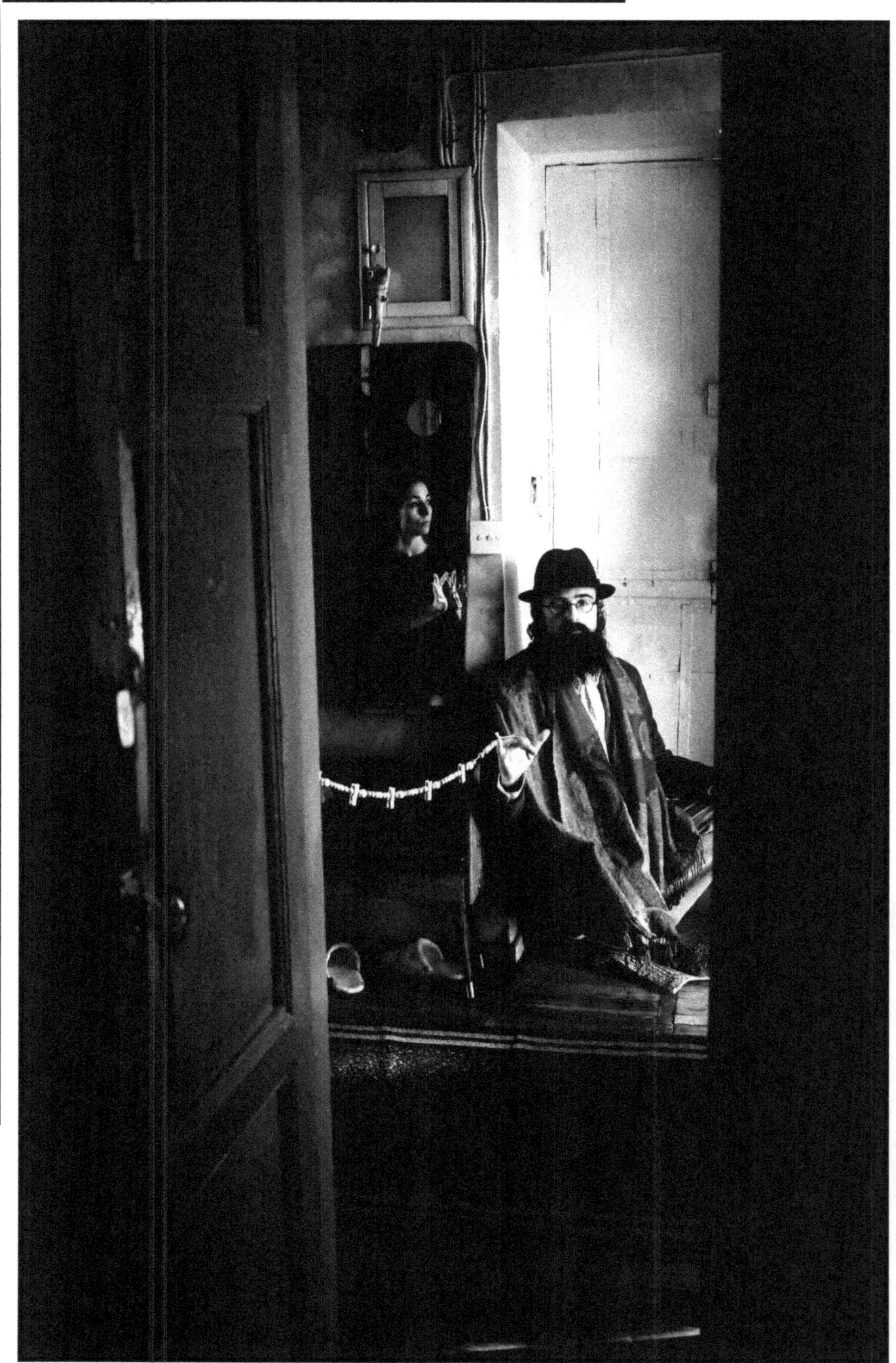

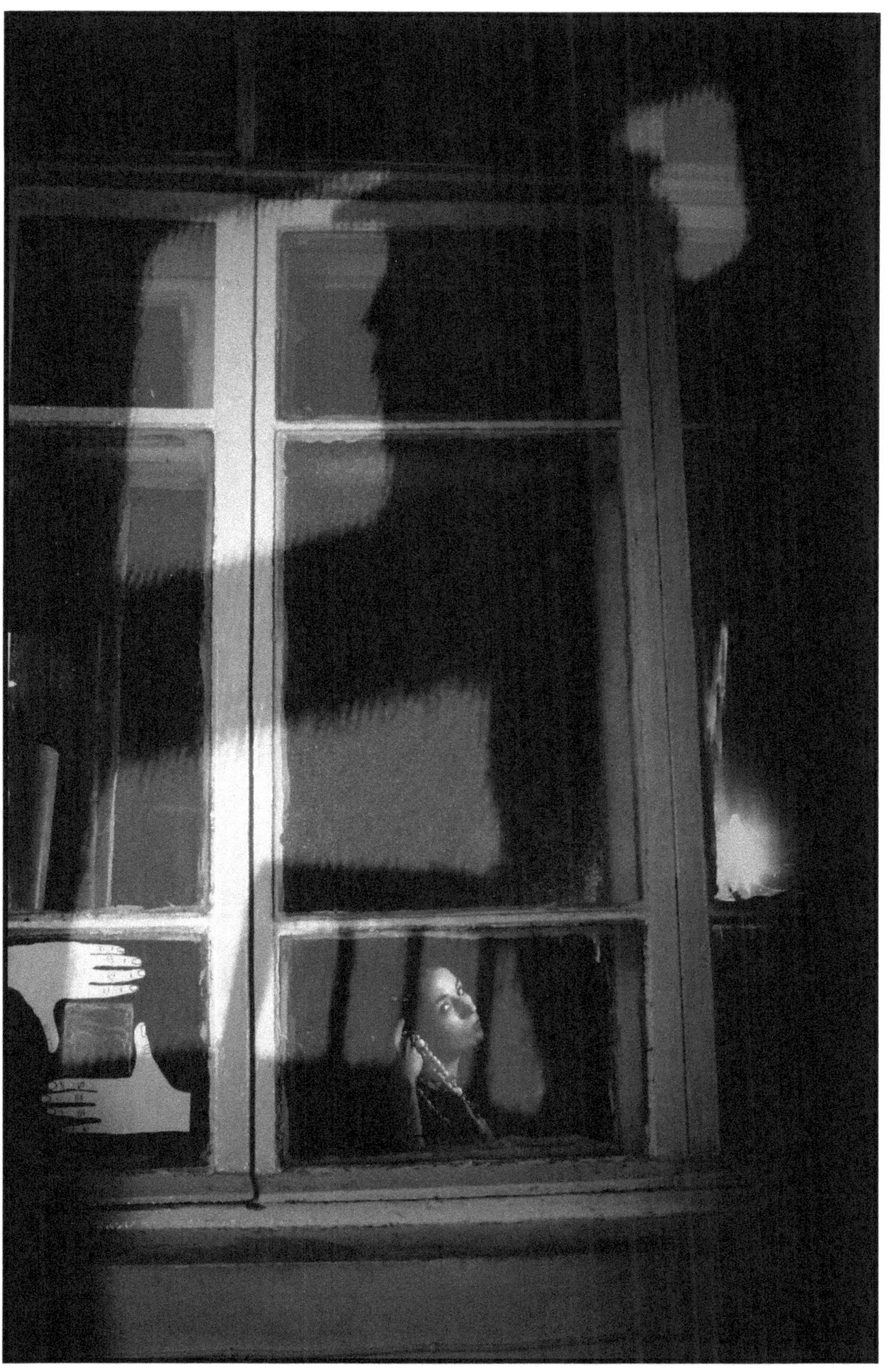

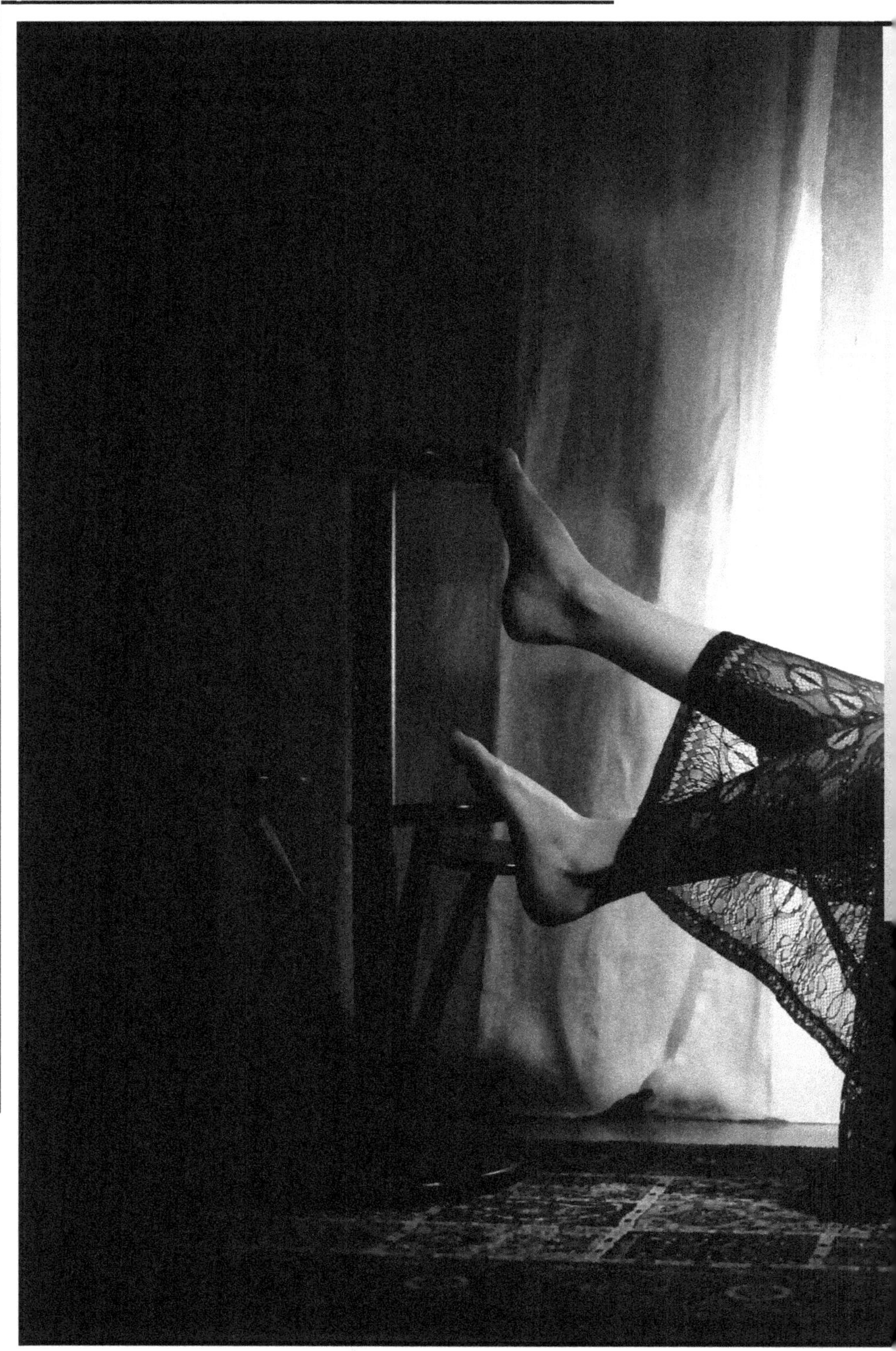

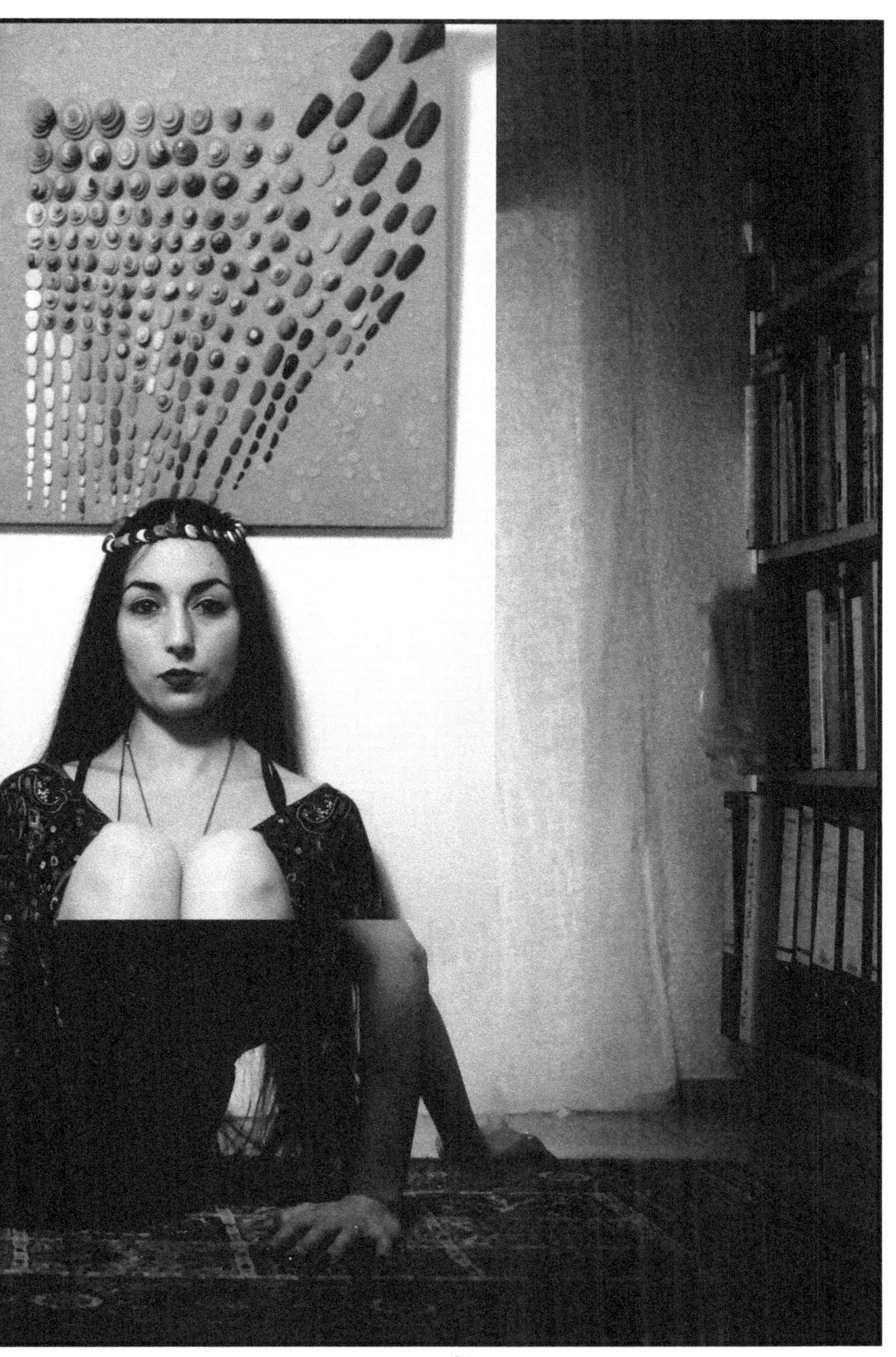

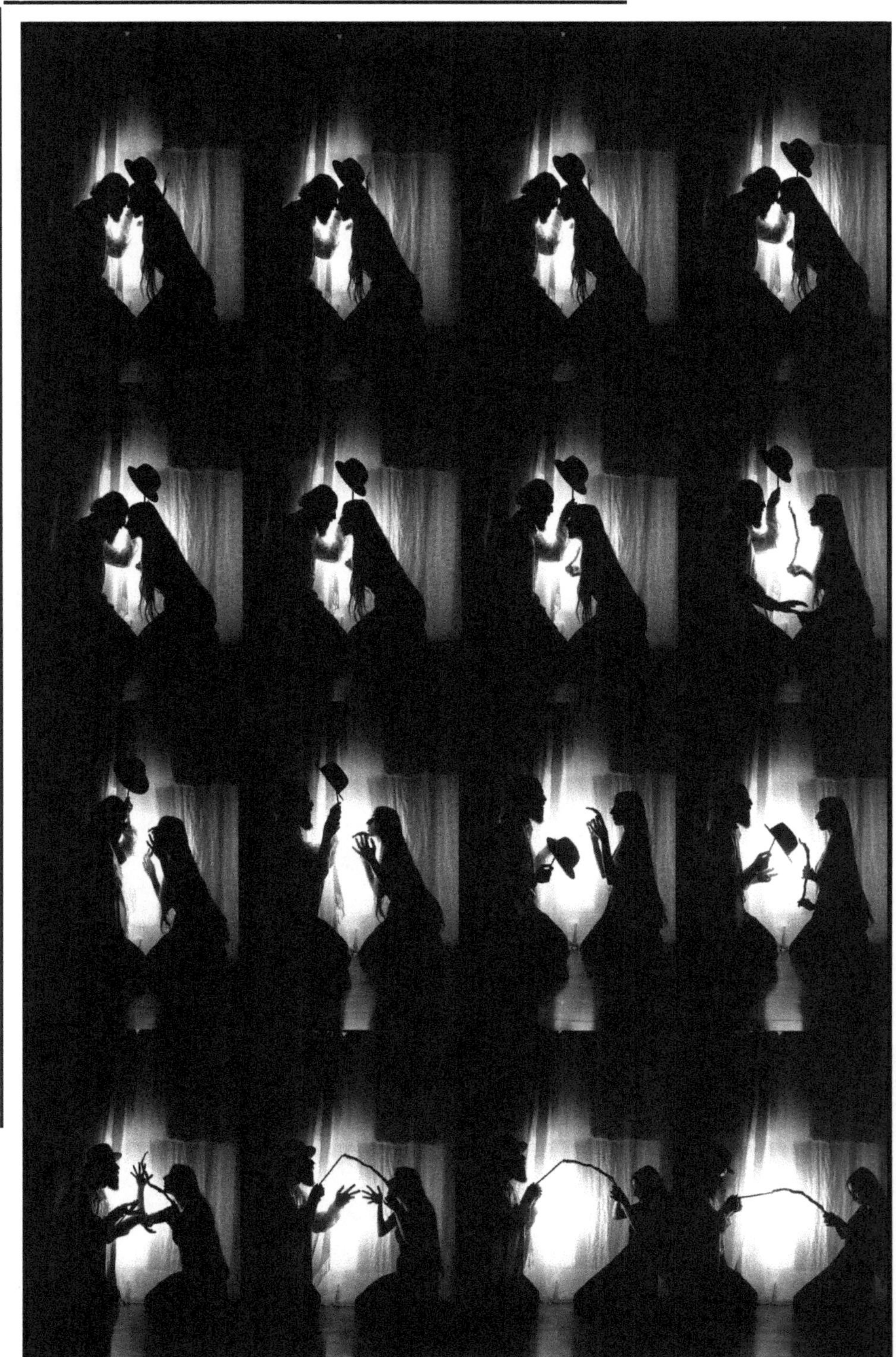

The friendly monster

Khaled K.E.M.

Every night I have the same dream,
my teeth are falling into the monster's lap.
One night I lost all of my teeth.
I could not speak.
I could not scream.
The monster feels sorry for me.
He asks me to bite him as hard as I can.
I signal how
now that I have no teeth.
The monster asks me to use my imagination,
my hatred,
my self-destruction,
my abomination.
I smile and tap on his shoulders
refusing such an offer.
When he insists
I tell him the story of the little boy
swallowed by his pet, the fat snake.
All night long the monster weeps in my arms,
and every time the void awakens him,
he brushes my teeth
and tearfully eats a part of me.

Infinity Mirror Rooms

Caroline Weinroth

After Yayoi Kusama

I.
"Your eye is a universe,"
I say to him, as the morning sunrise
splatters the sheets in his bedroom.
My body is close to the window
and it is translucent; my double
floats naked in glass.
He groans, "Your eye is a polka dot,"
and rolls over on to his side,
away from the window,
and me.

II.
I stand in his bathroom, door closed.
My plastic lashes, still by the sink.
Scrounge through my purse for some
make-up or glue, and unsnap a compact
of powder. My polka dot eye, naked, reflects
in the lid. Snap-close. I open his right-side
medicine cabinet and see its door
catch the light on the opposite
mirror; a vortex born on the wall.
Two mirrors, creating infinity.

III.
I enter a room of infinities.
Mirrors see mirrors see me see myself
in the mirrors, just me (and two windows).
If I had a companion, a romantic
passion, he could poke his head
through one window hole and I through the other
and we'd see each other, and only each other,
our eyes reflecting, lights flashing on faces
forever, love ever, forever in love, just our faces
long lasting and flashing in love.

IV.
I exit all rooms alone.

lunar voyage

Andrée-Anne Guay

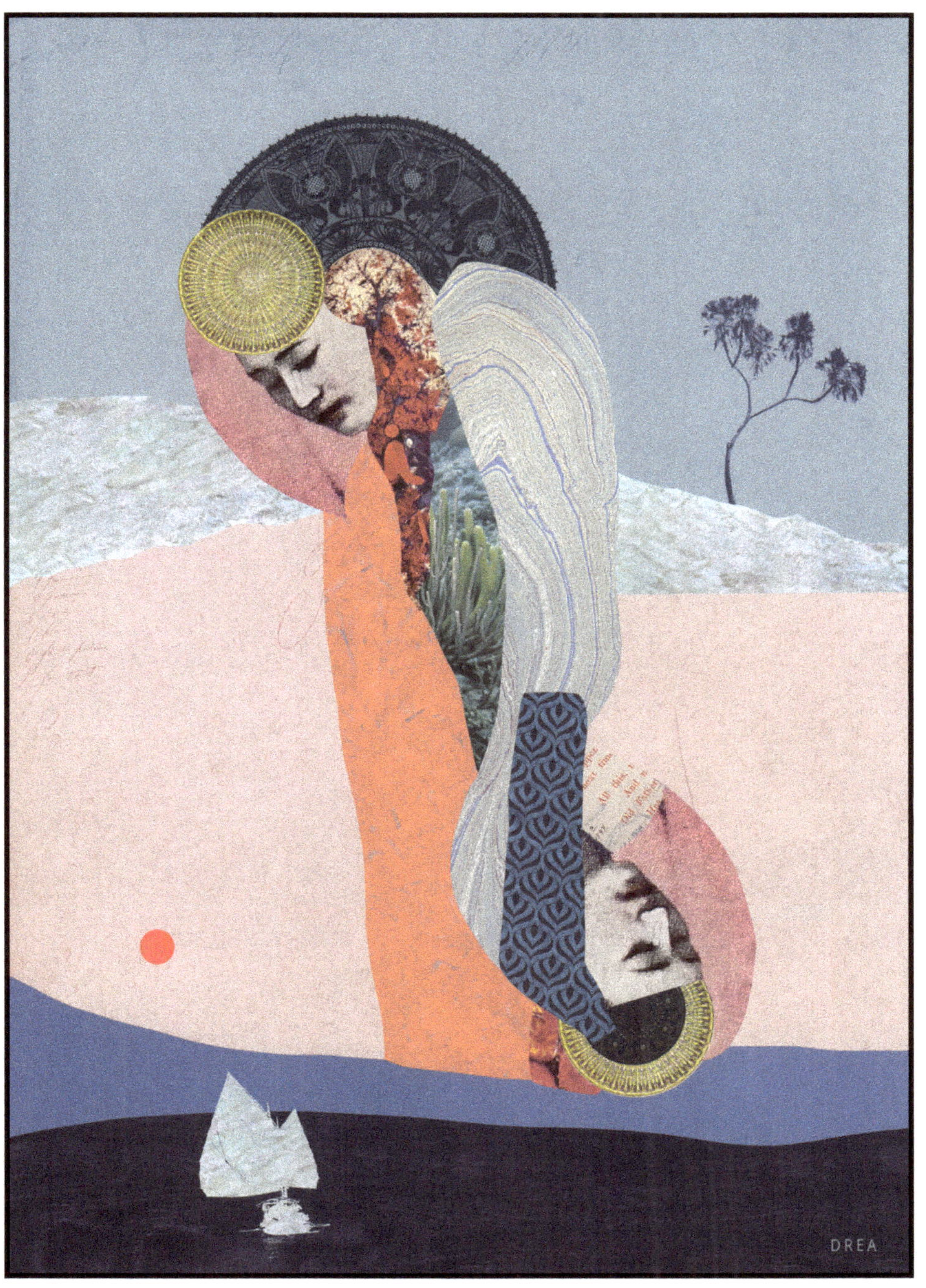

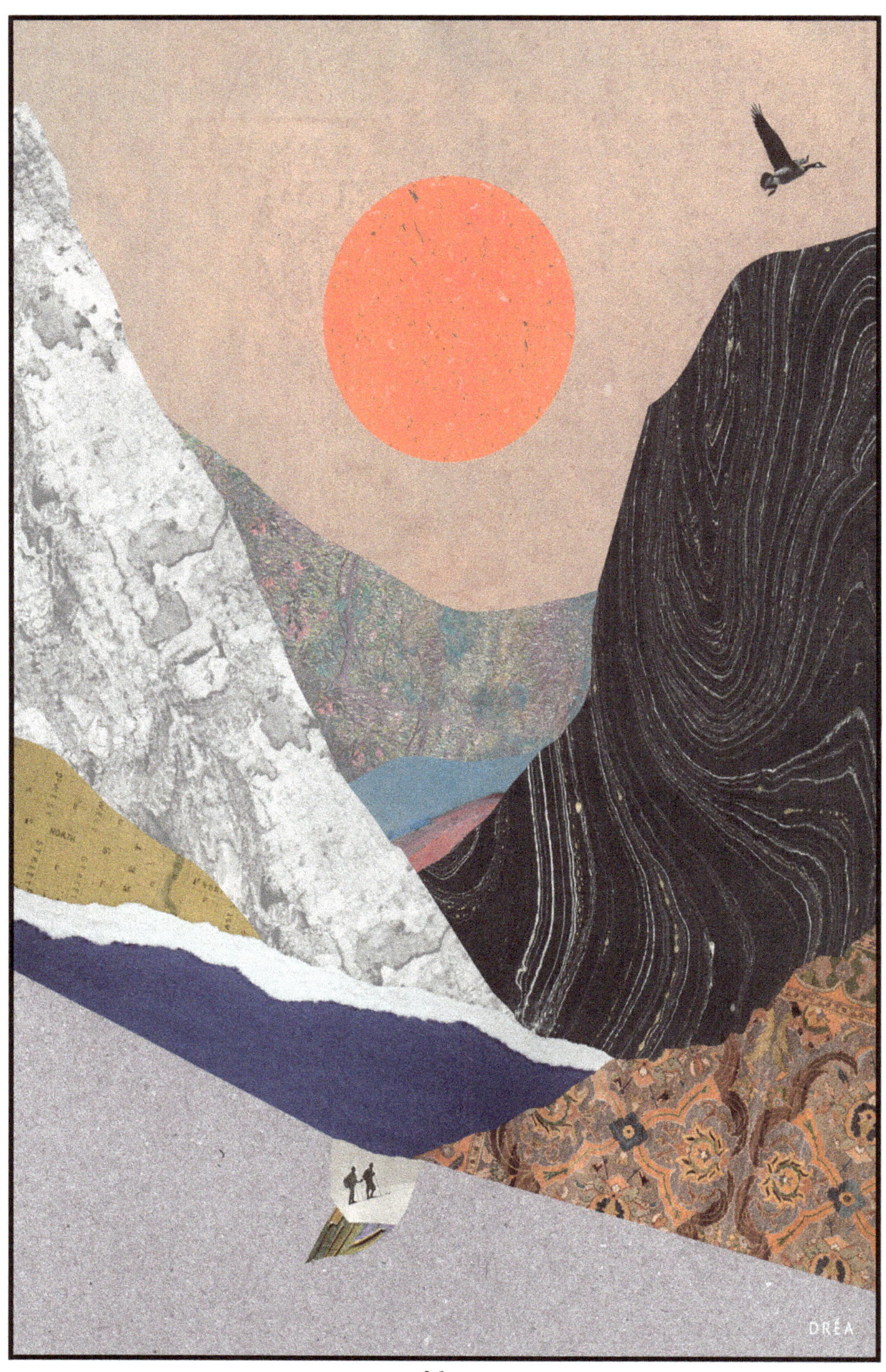
DRÉA

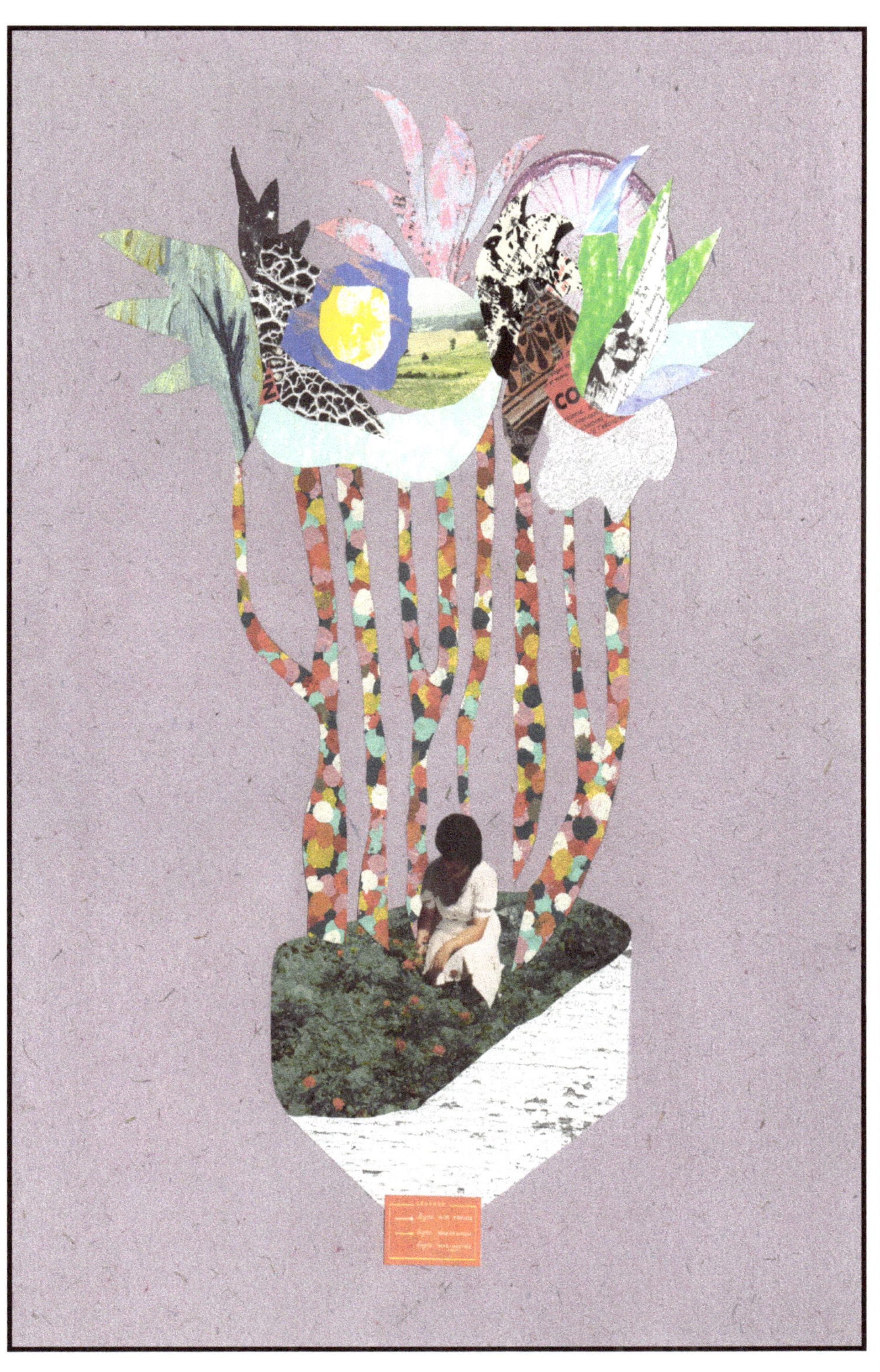

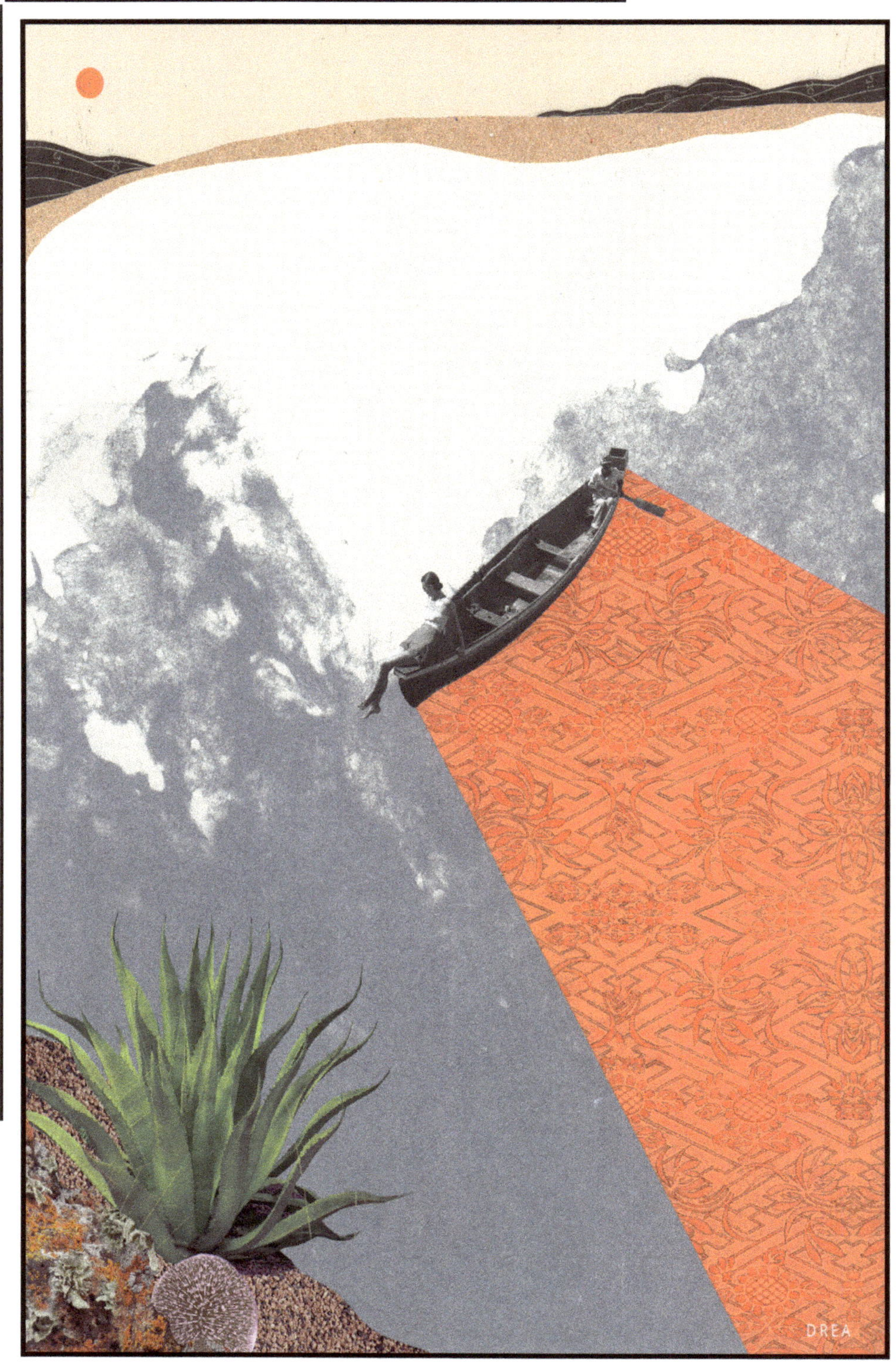
DREA

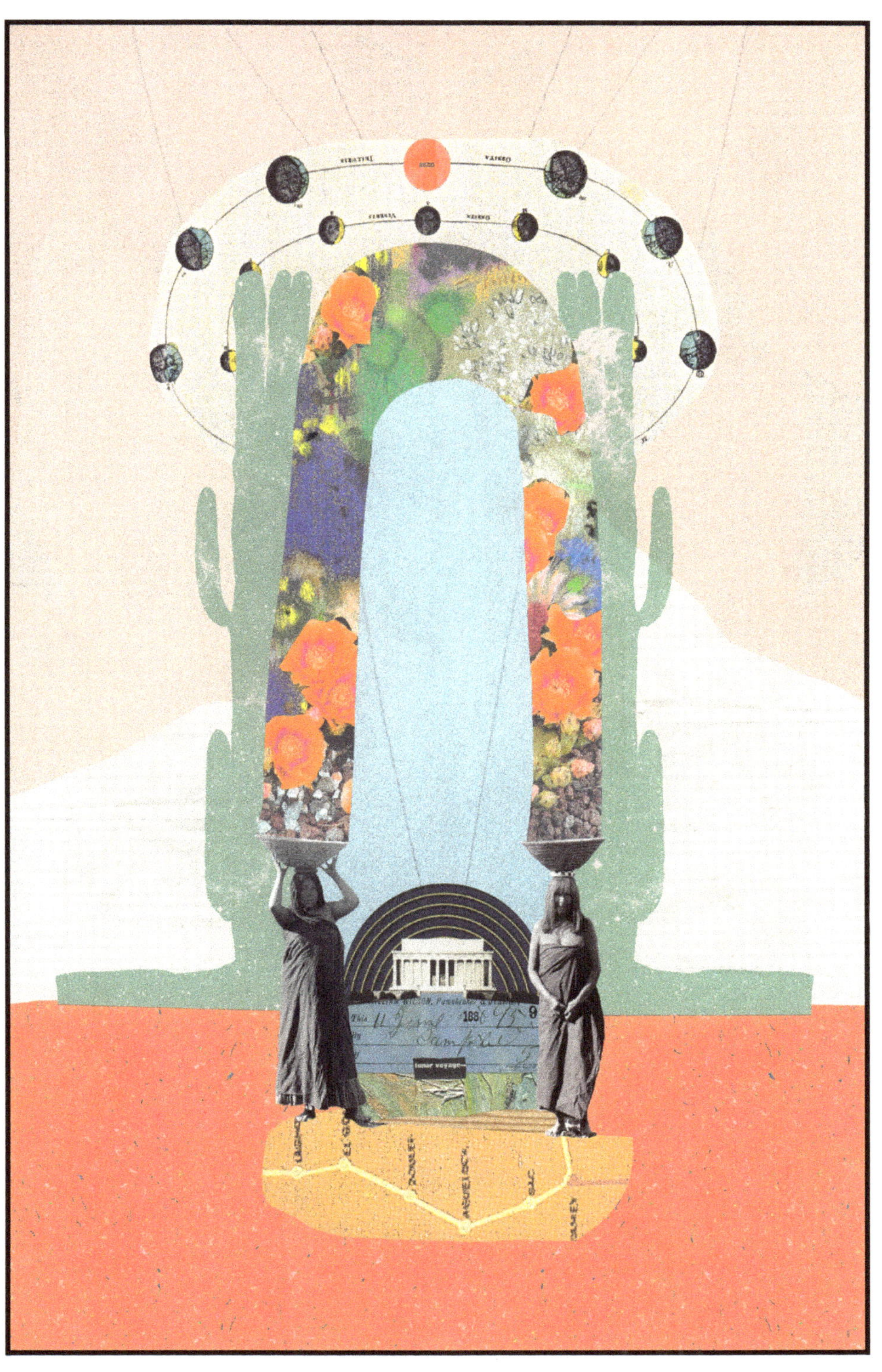
lunar voyage—

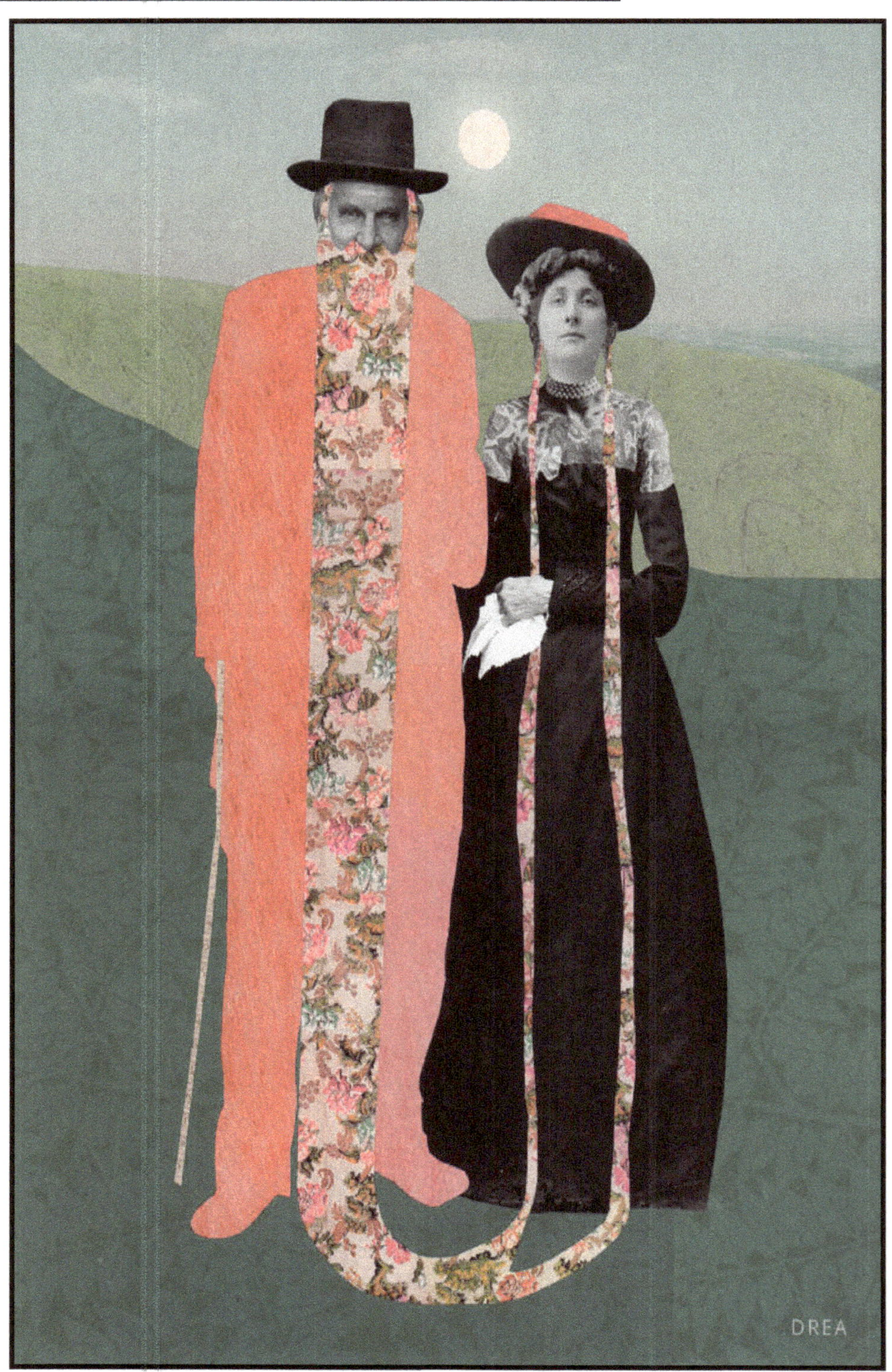
DREA

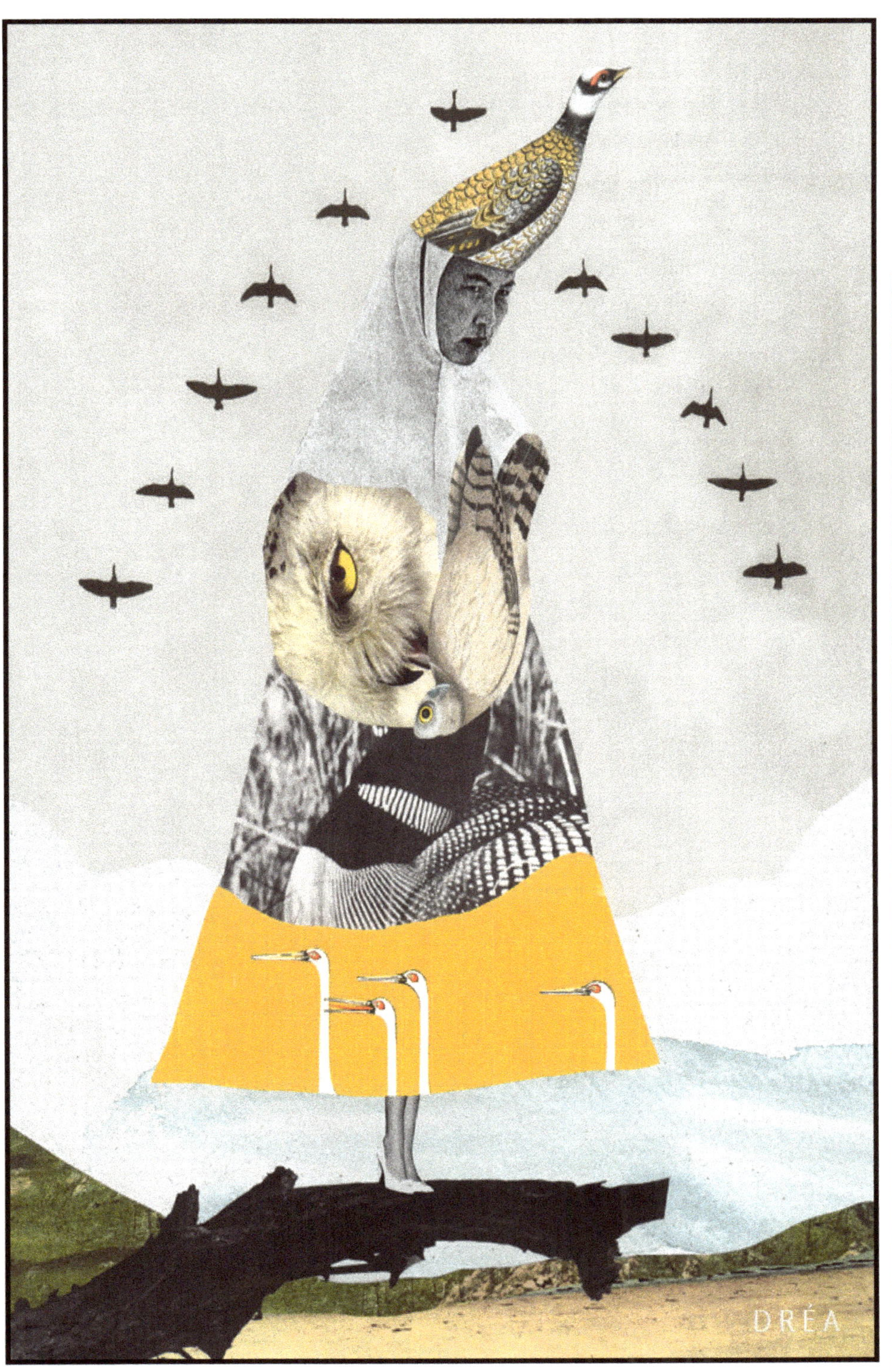
DRÉA

Hollywood Park

Jonathan Yungkans

Follow the clue patiently and you will find nothing.
—Basil Bunting, "Briggflats"

Nothing was darkness, taut as rope or reins
that threatened to pull from my hands, cut

a straight line across palms till they bled.
Just the betting floor where I now walked

felt solid, a polished, faint glimmer.
You'd think the seats or track would seem real,

where spectators cheered their bets to run
faster than money from their wallets

while the mounts on turf pursued the wind
for the unbridled joy of catching it,

born to persist. They had chased themselves,
invisible to all but mind's eye,

into memory; the glow itself,
caught from the infield, was a specter,

even if I was the only one
haunting the place. Over the track, clouds

stretched, a tight-knit pack down the back stretch,
crowding the north turn—as though spirits

of horses in nothing's perceptible calm
who refused to wait—airstream pulling

stratocumuli into muscle,
channeled in leather between fingers.

•

"Another time"—my mom's sole comment
over the phone, no explanation

or facial expression—glass bottle's
clarity, filled with milk, unopened—

the kindness of her opacity.
(Nor did I know then the container

had cracked deep, swallowed into white
silence—a family trait?) This was

months after my walk, the morning
the park—the otherness of what was

and wasn't home—had been dynamited,
grandstand undulated like a wave,

ocean groaning into air, only
to fall back onto itself. No hint

if the subject itself too fragile,
like Adohr Farms bottles at our door

when I was young—half-gallons like those
I keep in my refrigerator

That, once frozen, shatter into long,
lacerating flakes or memories. Was

another time the fire that galloped,
thick-muscled as the Black Stallion,

seen as far as San Pedro? The blaze
that brought Pappy, my great-grandfather,

to rebuild grandstand, clubhouse, all
reduced to ashes and air—nothing.

•

My footsteps bounced their measured cadence
back at me, resonant. Dimness masked

roof, support columns, walls—what he helped
reconstruct, wood and metal he touched;

only staccato concrete confirmed
my existence—the nonentity

that also substantiated him—
his hush, always letting the tools speak.

•

We shared building, our work days a clean,
sharp lined blue-print: his khaki long sleeves

cap, trousers, spread-only sandwiches
that kept him lanky but fed; his words,

whenever he hurt himself working,
"Job's no good without some blood on it."

Pappy had me haul, stack lumber scraps
for firewood, the wheelbarrow's handles

thick, rough wooden arms that felt attached
extensions of my own, time heavy,

depending on the load's balance, how
high the expectations, the stacked length

of two-by-fours for framing walls—nailed,
cross-braced—their rattle-slap when wheeled.

•

Pacing, all my thoughts rolled together,
I followed variances of light

for the hidden clues inside me—hardware
like the bent nails Pappy kept, straightened,

put in jelly jars; shelved in his garage
like the rushed words I could sometimes catch

and put into something workable
despite my brain's mad dash, stopwatched past

my mile-and-a-quarter. Gravity
brings grief across a headstone's stiffness,

between hoofbeats and watchworks' tick held
in hand—one pulse against another.

•

Another time, ocean, undertow,
circular— hands around a watch face,

lunar in unchanging insistence.
Overnight at Grandma and Pappy's,

Pappy would stop the grandfather clock—
stilled the pendulum and left. Never

said why. Didn't miss a night. Tucked in
the hide-a-bed, I watched him walk,

silent, deliberate as time itself,
stop that clock, leave. Then it was morning.

•

At the park, a watch tick in footfalls,
slowed but sharp as pencil marks on wood.

Where to mark, though? What part of me falls
when my thoughts dig like hooves into turf

when mania hems me in, a race pack
that runs until heart or legs give out?

Words fly in clods, kicked up, yet it's hard
to mention sanity's chase, its arc

like a pendulum bob minus its rod
to keep me from landing on the track—

or a beam's split end, sawn, to hit ground
with a *thunk*, good only for firewood.

Pappy made quietness look too easy.
Now I wonder if the touch was his

for complete solace, or what weights pulled
inside a walnut cabinet, how tight

his mainspring wound. Was his tension mine?
His spindles? Wheels and gears turned us both,

surreptitious behind glass—
another race's thunder in blood,

obscured in khaki and hammering—
arcs that drove nails, held the mind in place

and hold it now as it follows clouds
which jockey full-speed for position.

Veronica's Cloths

K. Johnson Bowles

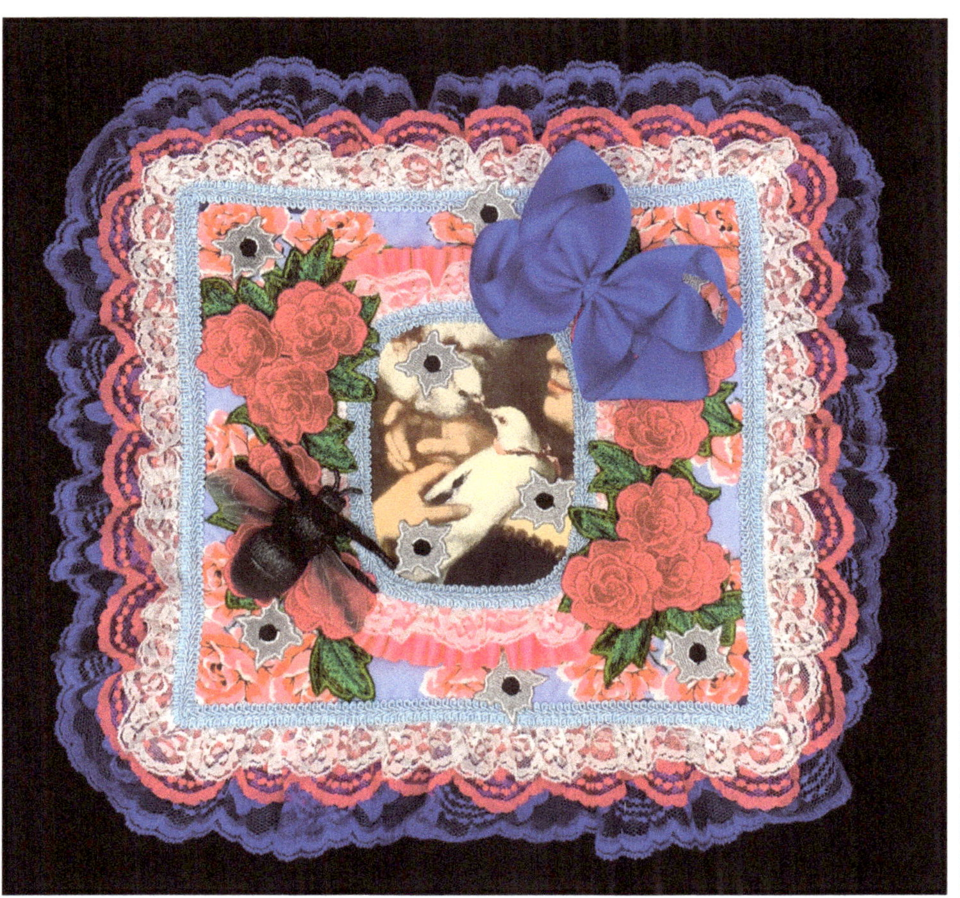

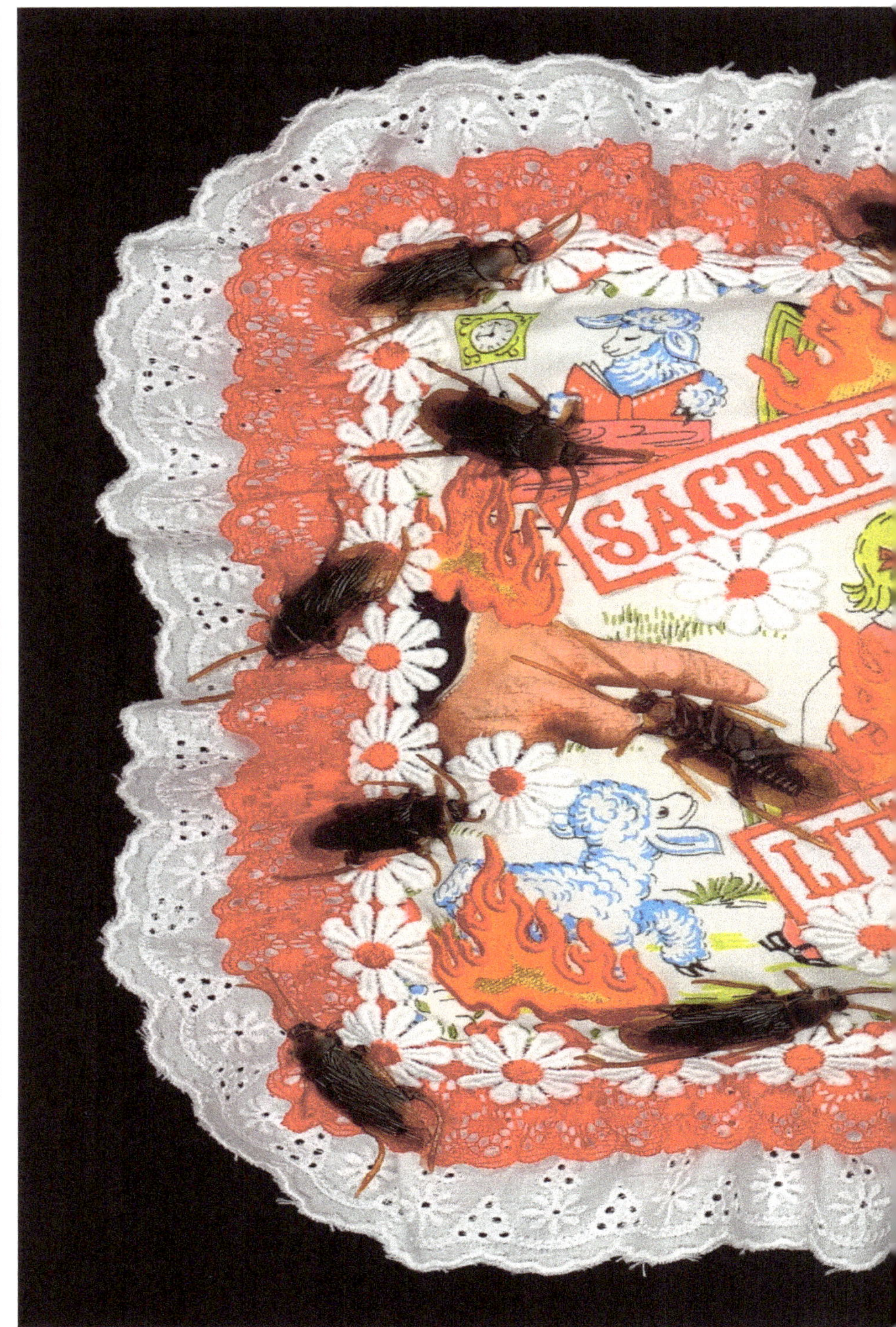

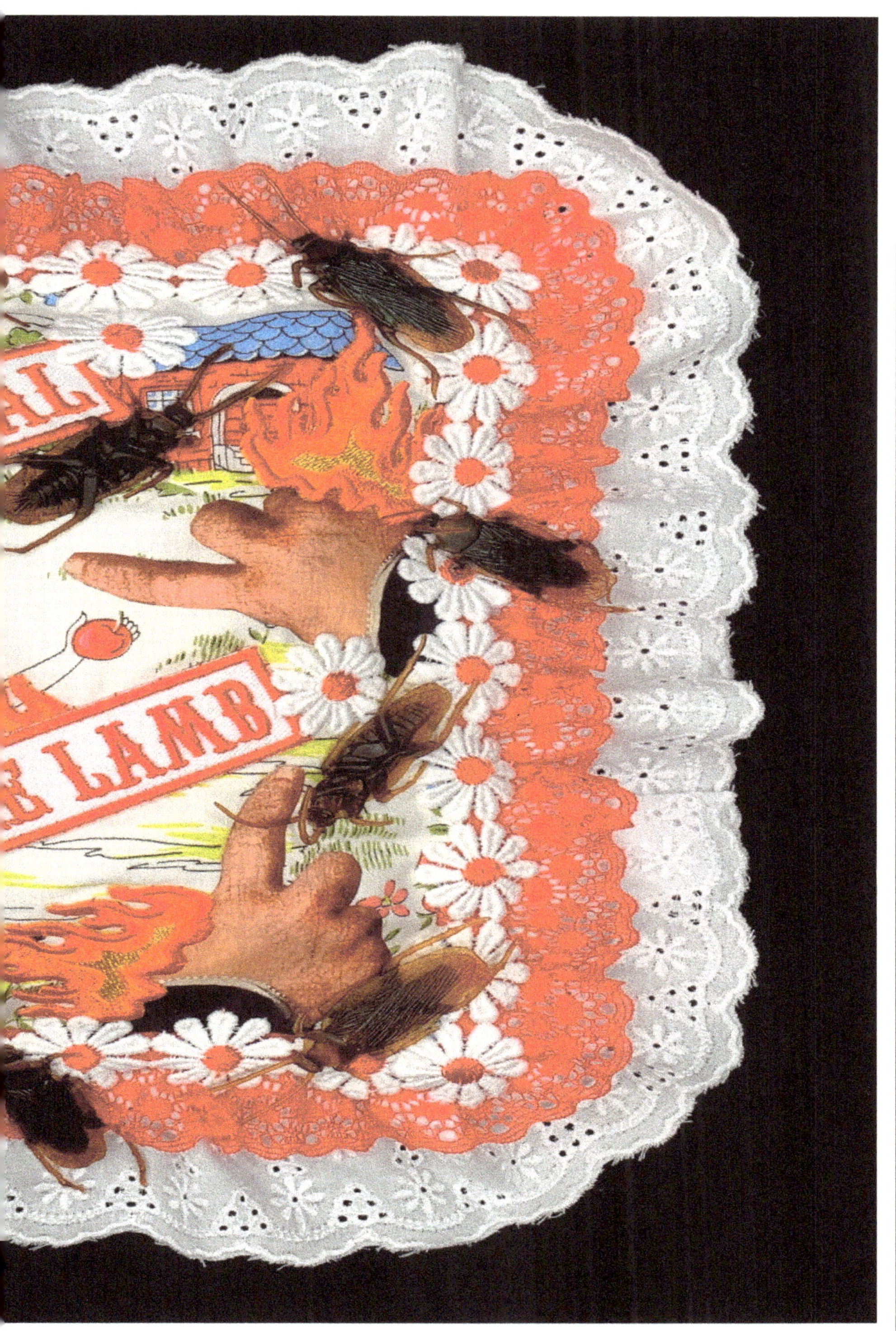
LAMB

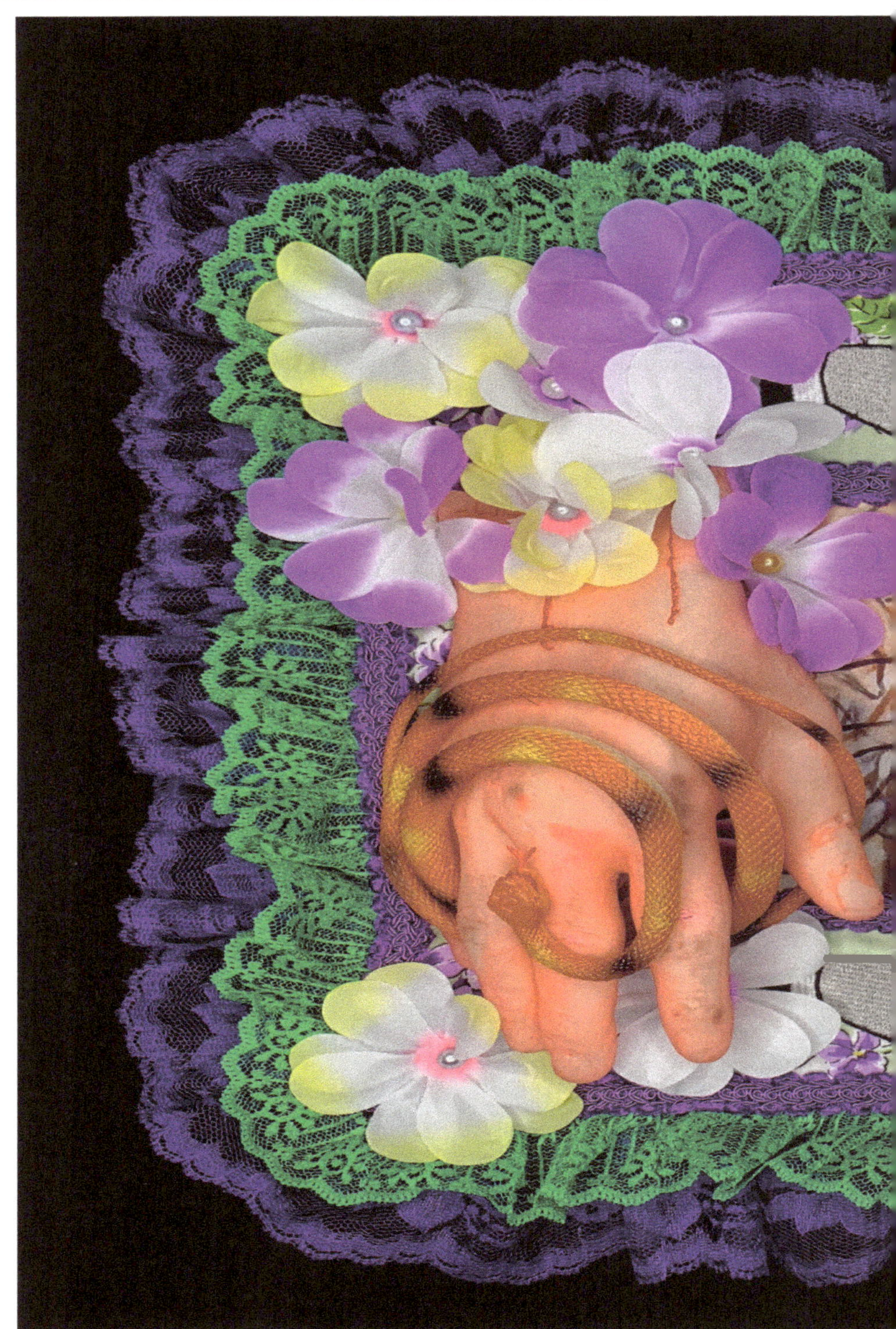

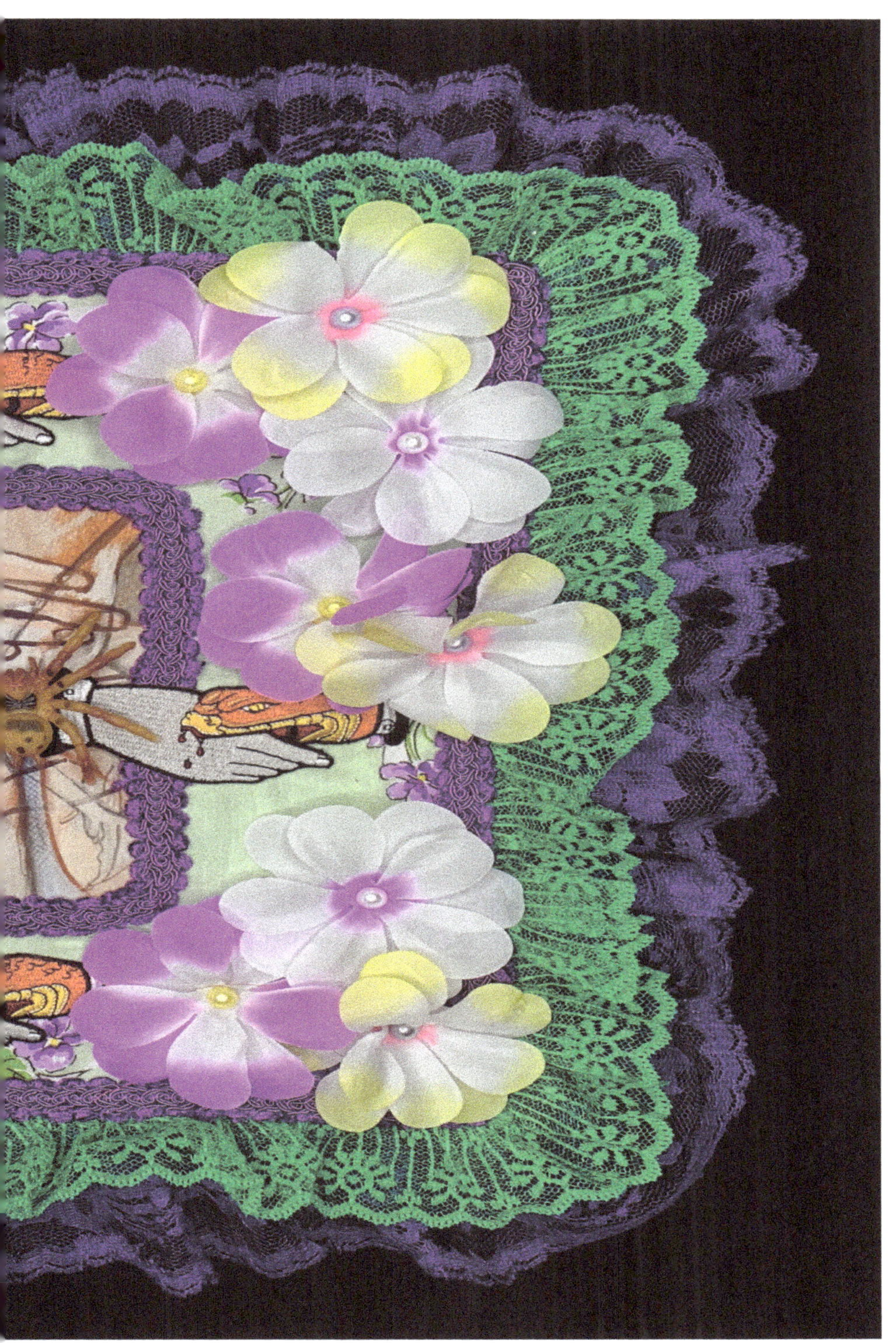

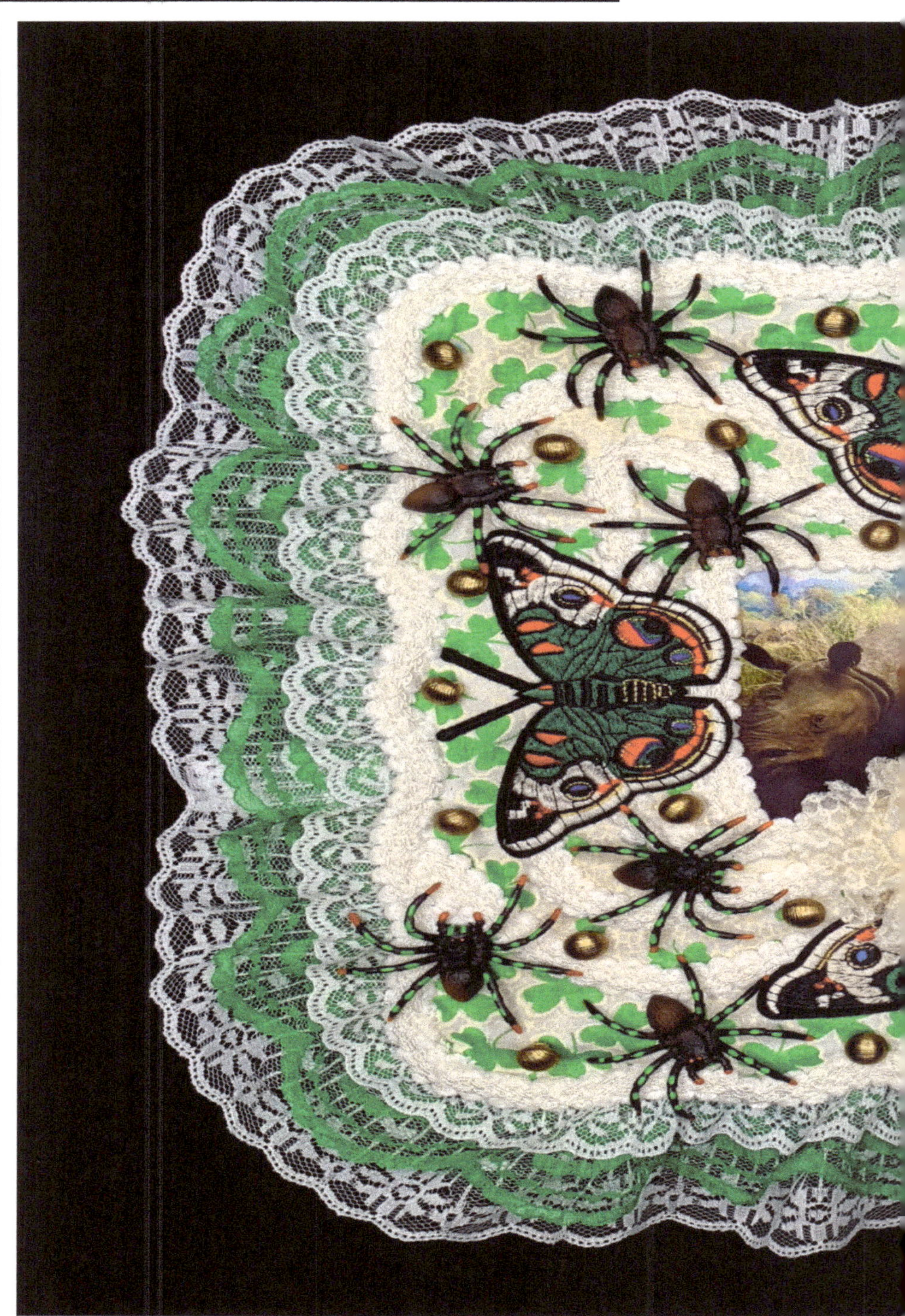

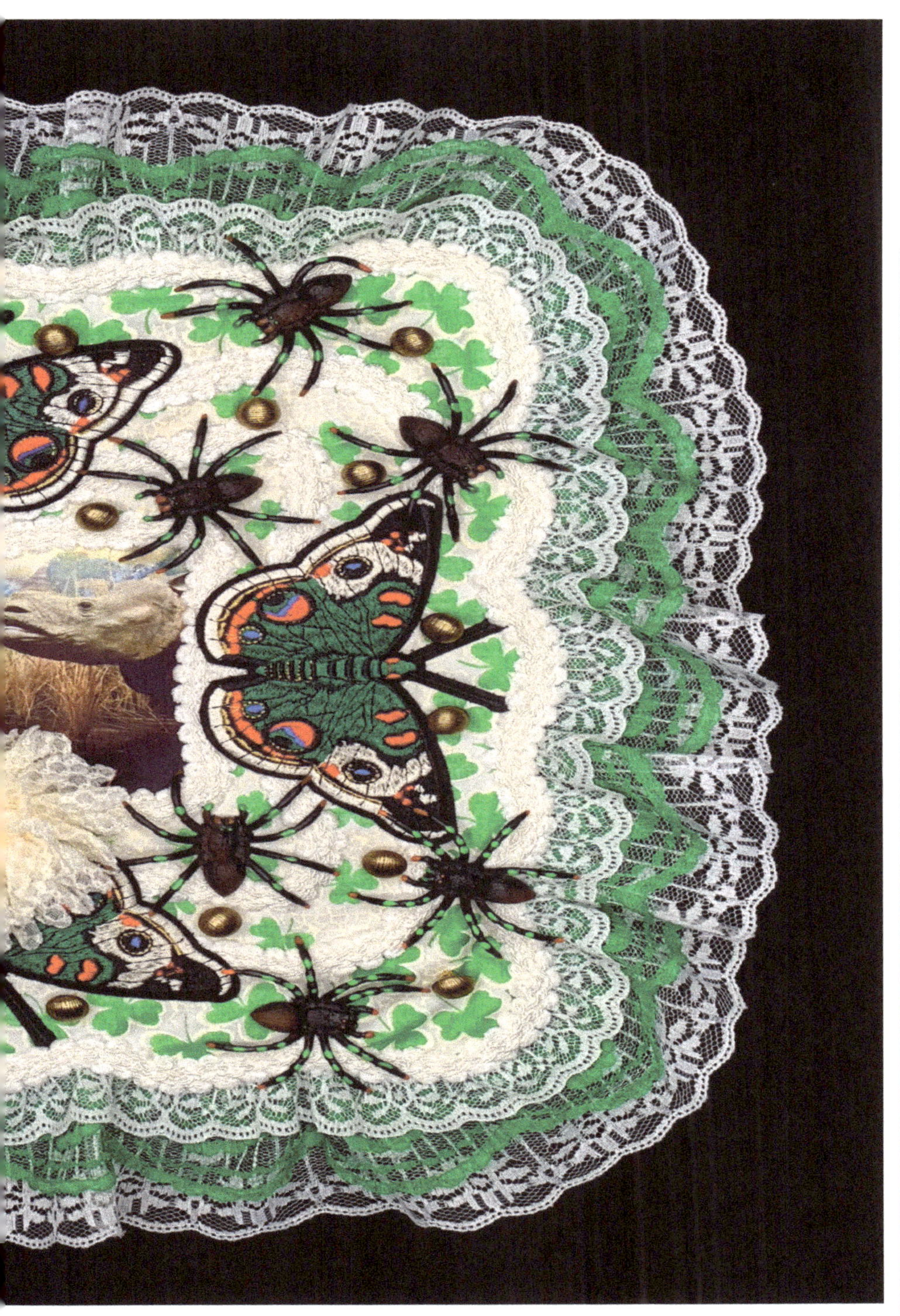

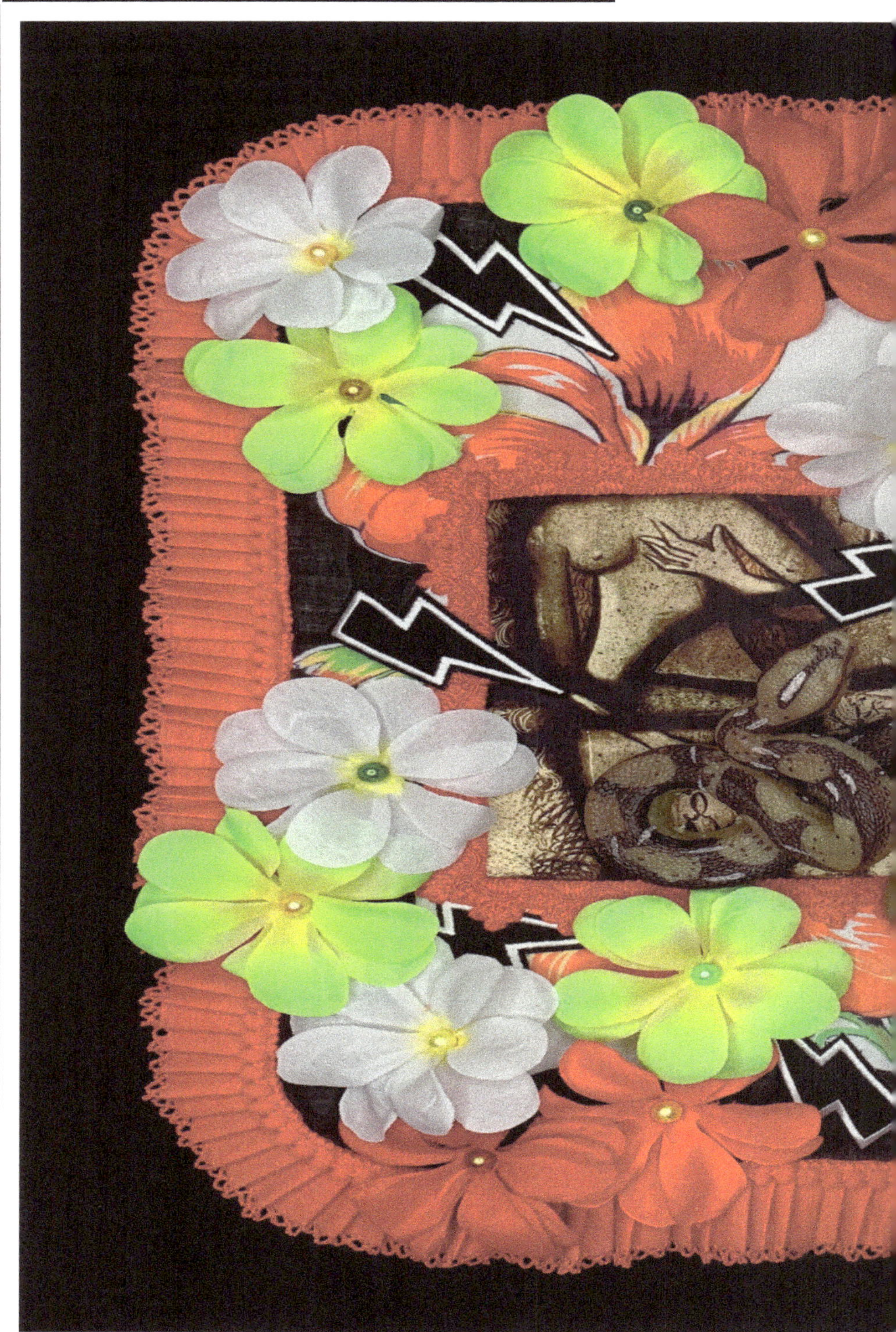

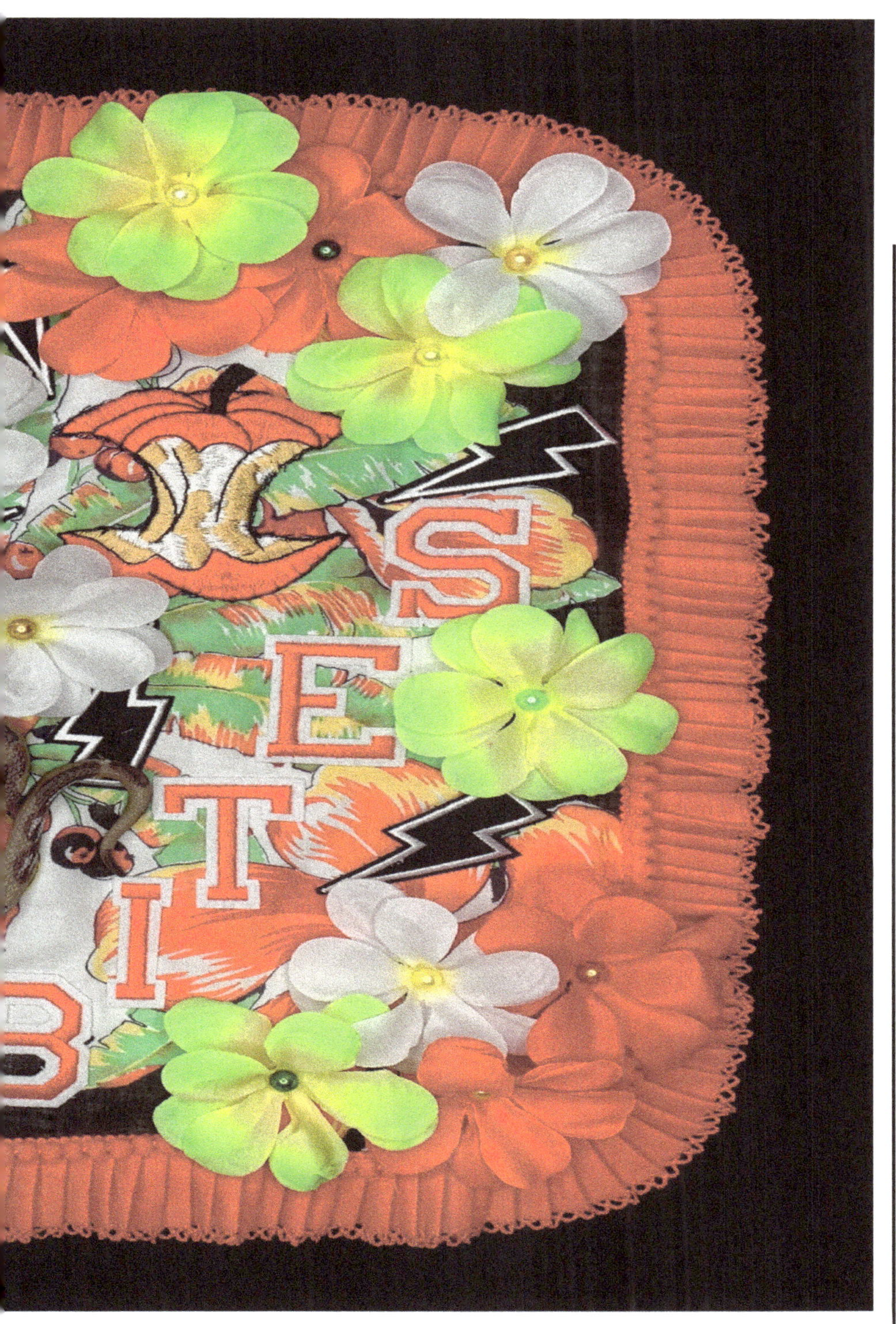
BITES

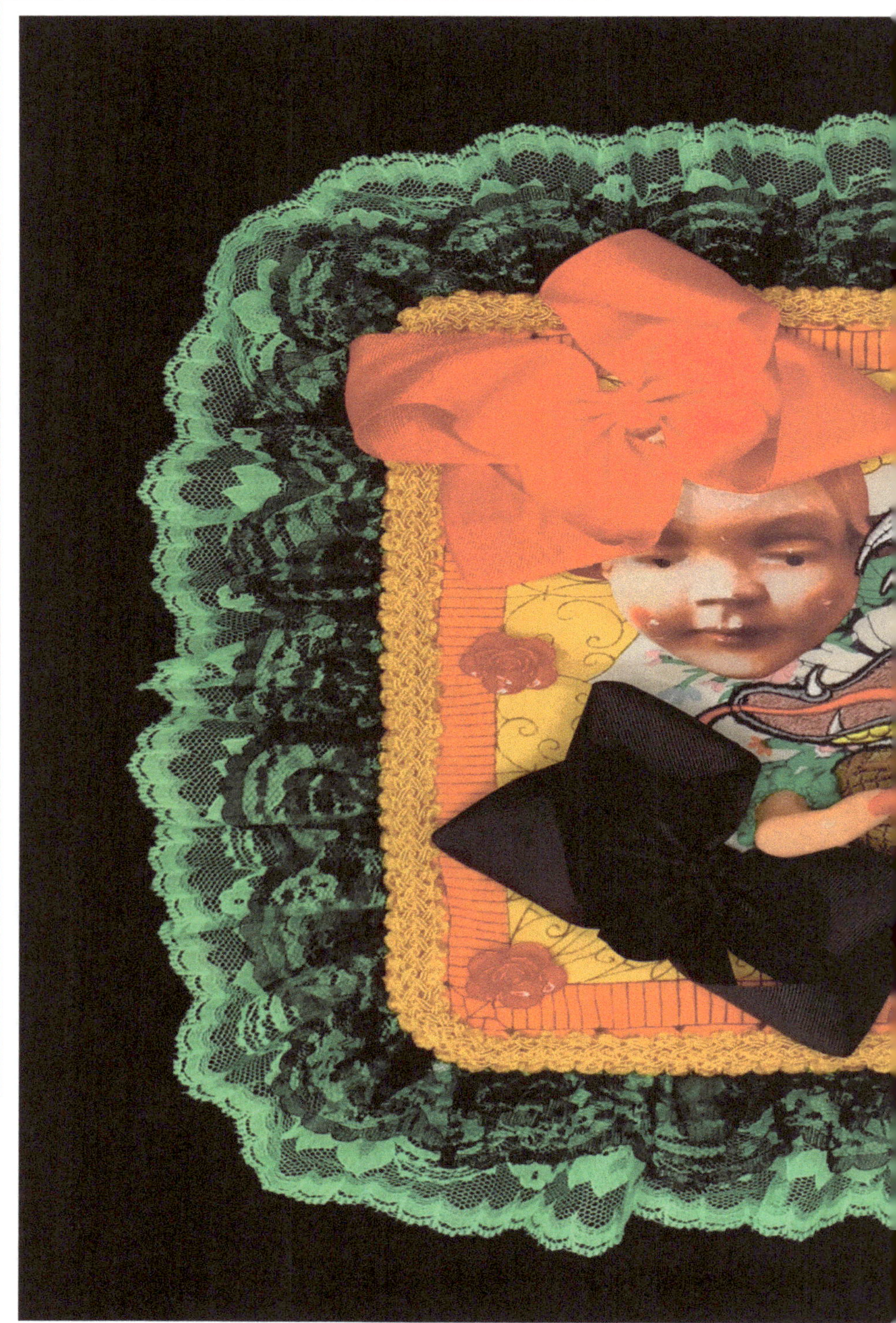

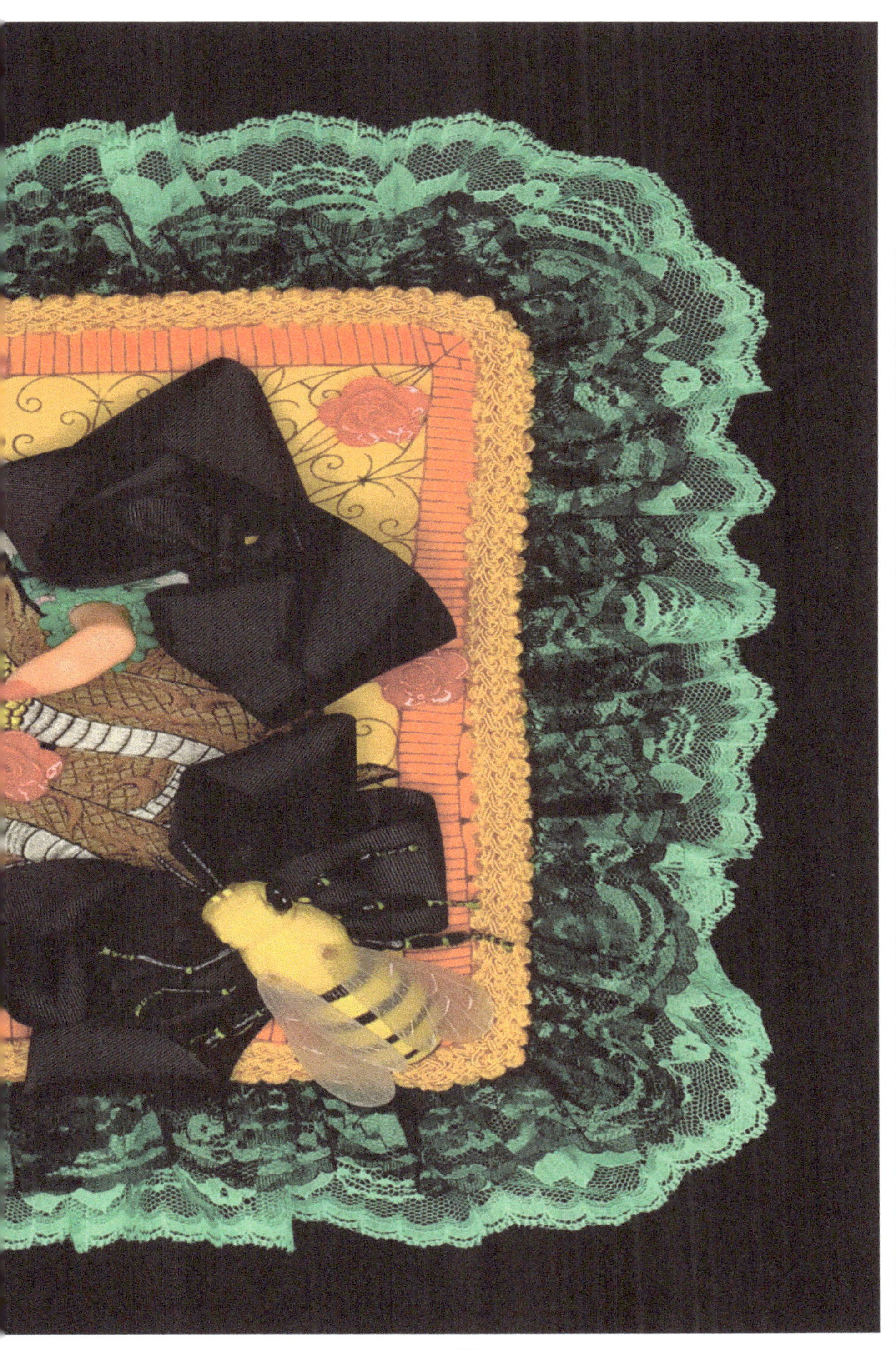

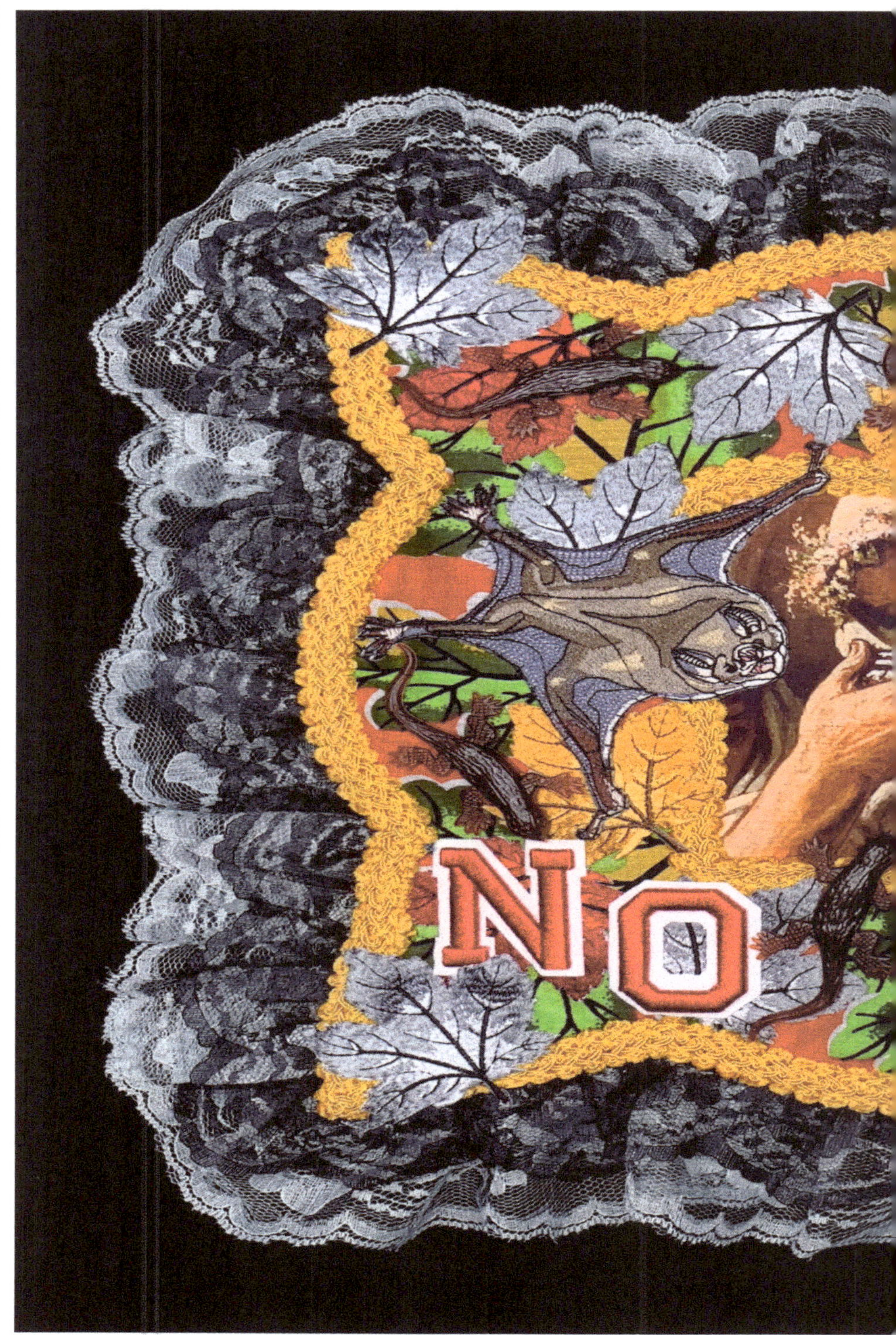
NO

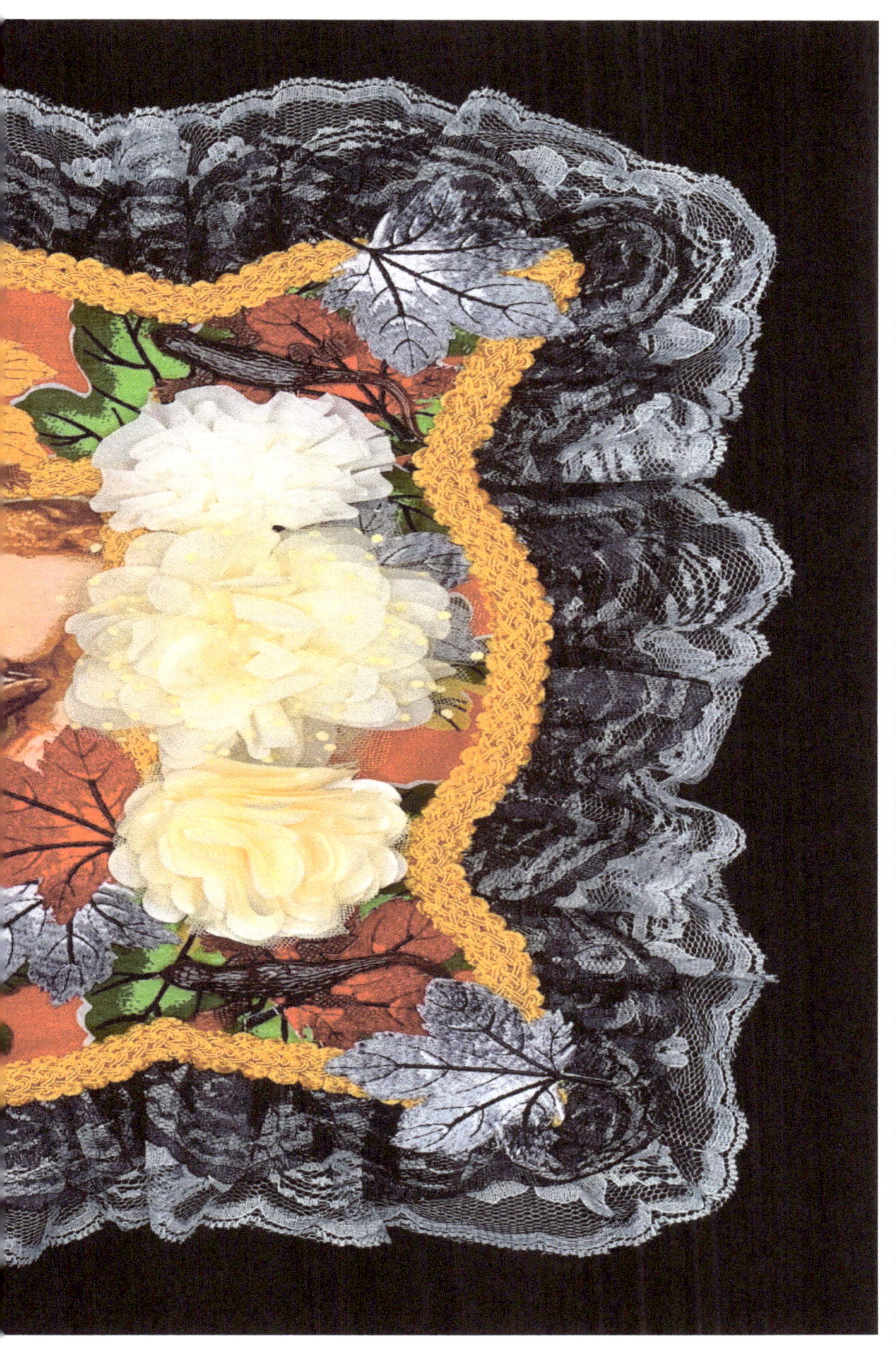

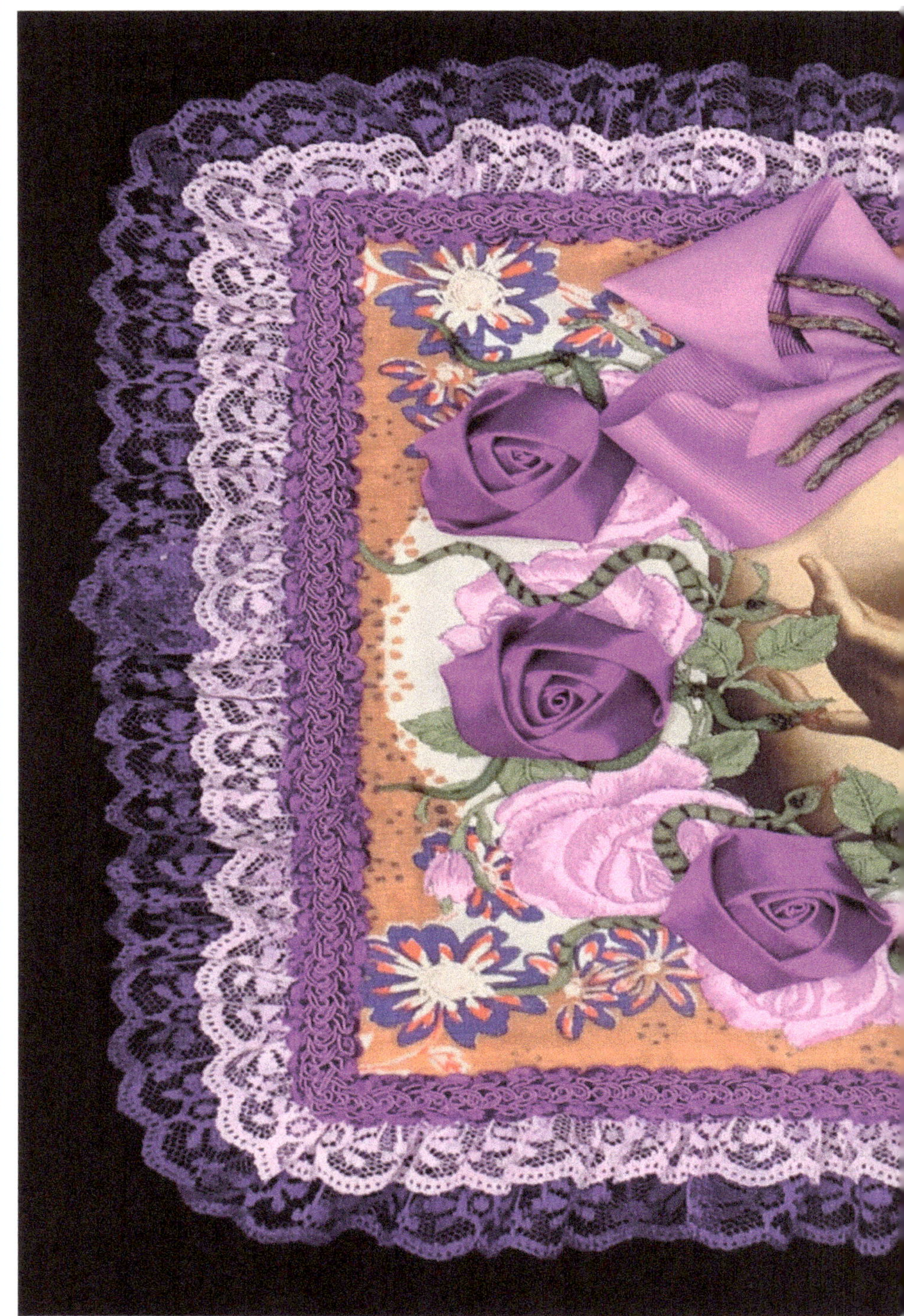

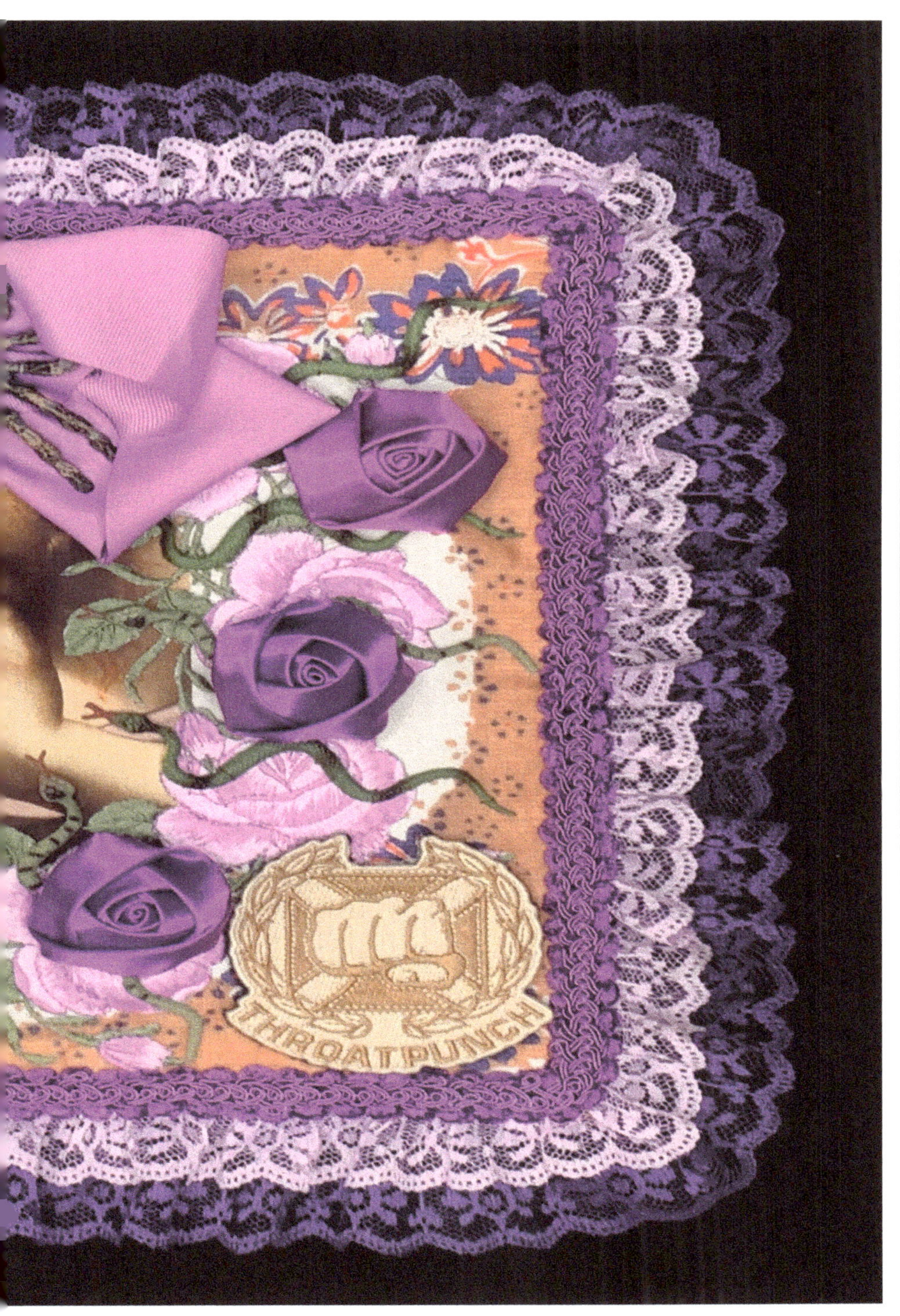
THROATPUNCH

Two Days (Dog Days)

Jeremy James George

Thursday

Sitting alone on my back porch, my wife & kids still asleep—I don't remember if it is morning or midnight—first my neighbor's compressor & then ours kicked in, kicking on the AC, scaring a rabbit out of hiding. There had been desolation, a knowledge in the quiet, disrupted. The sky had been or was blue on blue.

/

We have one TV & it is on. The girls are watching something silly, about mermaids or flying unicorns or trolls. I am waiting, I don't like waiting, but I am waiting & waiting. I can't say for what, ex-actly, but I know it's something that struggles to get here, like light or darkness, like *goodbye*, like the first hour, like the final hour of summer.

/

I look up, up above the neighbor's house, & see three hawks hover & dart against the blue in yesterday's
blue, the blue of today, tomorrow.
I cough & no one hears me. It seems like I am always a little less than a line away from saying what I need to say.

Friday

I knew Van Gogh cut off his ear—he painted himself without it after all—though I didn't know he'd given it to a woman at half-eleven that same night & asked her to take good care of it. The stars, then, dissolved in two irreconcilable impastos.

If he had a plan it was a terrible plan or no plan—just survive the next hour & then the next.

/

Go to the community pool, make lunch, watch a cartoon, play dolls, build a Lego fortress. Something, anything, to pass the hours. Like someone somewhere whispering *doldrum* into the ear of the day.

/

Perhaps the question we need to ask ourselves, if not in despair, is what manner of self-portrait would we commission? &, just as importantly, what besides truth do we most need ignited?

Tuscan Red

Joe Pagano Jr.

Made inarticulate
by snowfall,
the wood surrounds us in silence.

Your small hand,
balled in my own, discerns
my pulse
like a rabbit in her warren
does the fox.

A gibbous moon
squats on the umber hill
like Bronzino's
Nano Morgante.

Apollo.

Neo-Romanti-Classics: Mythical Beauty

Adam Shea Lancaster

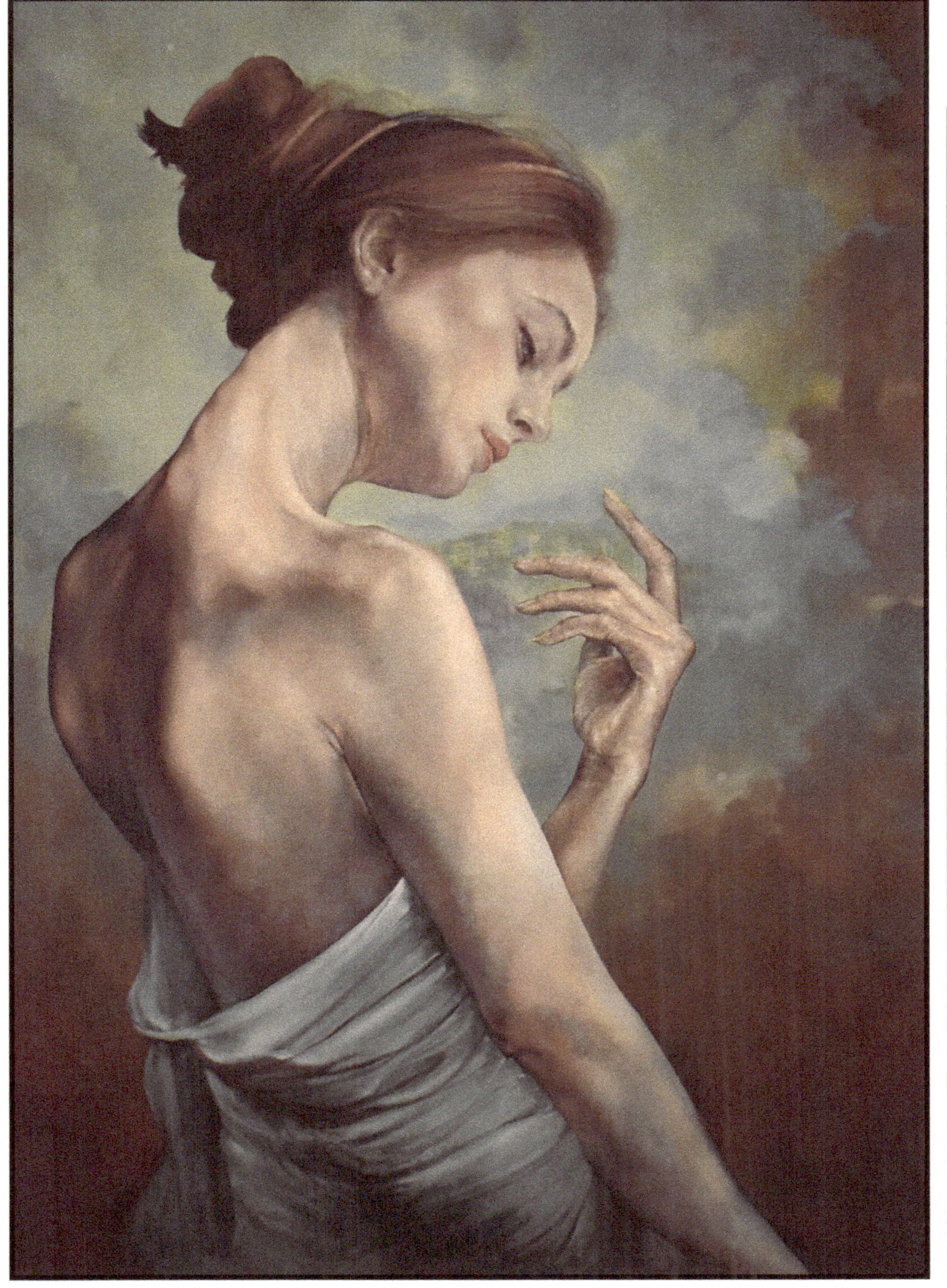

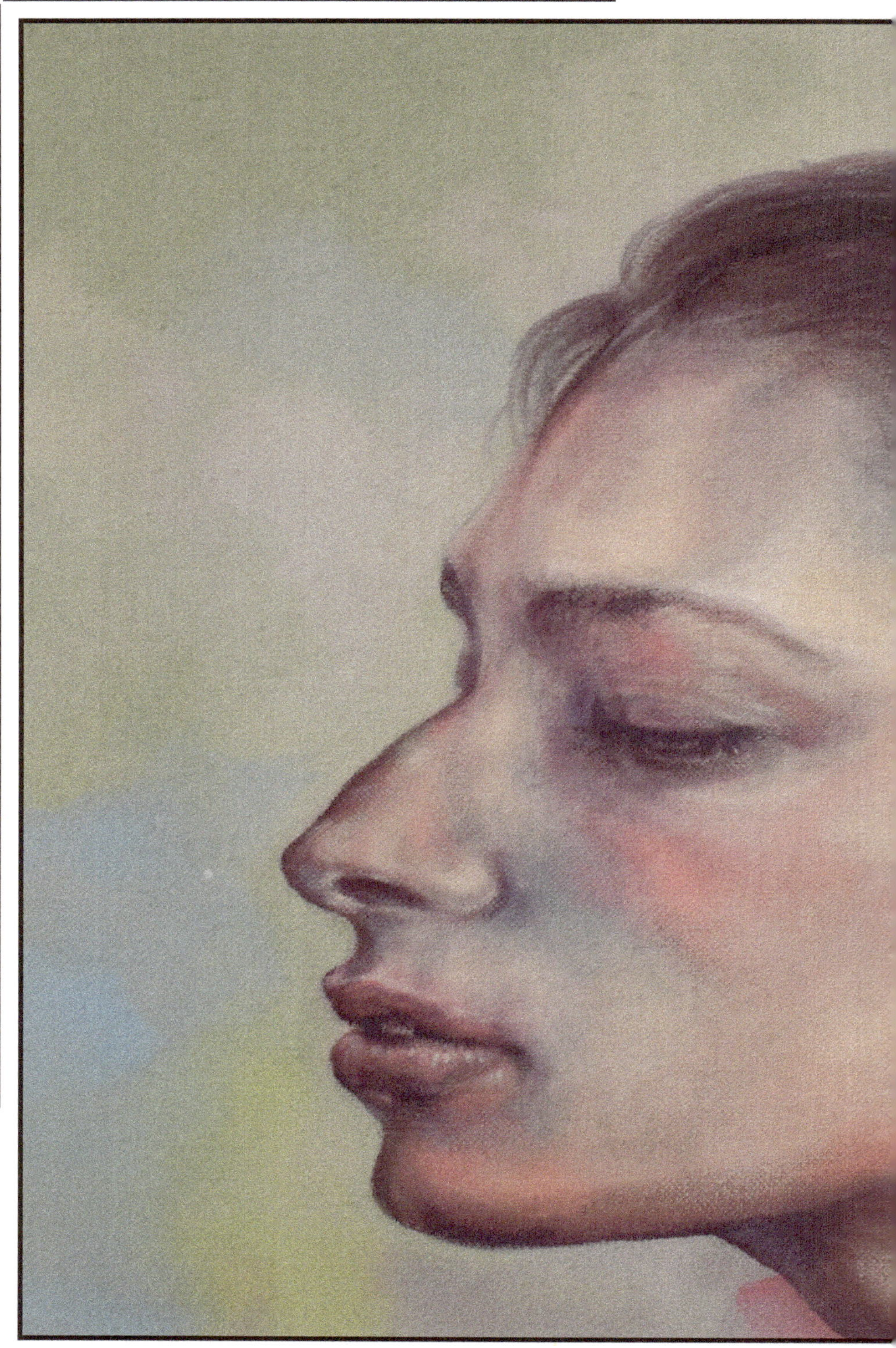

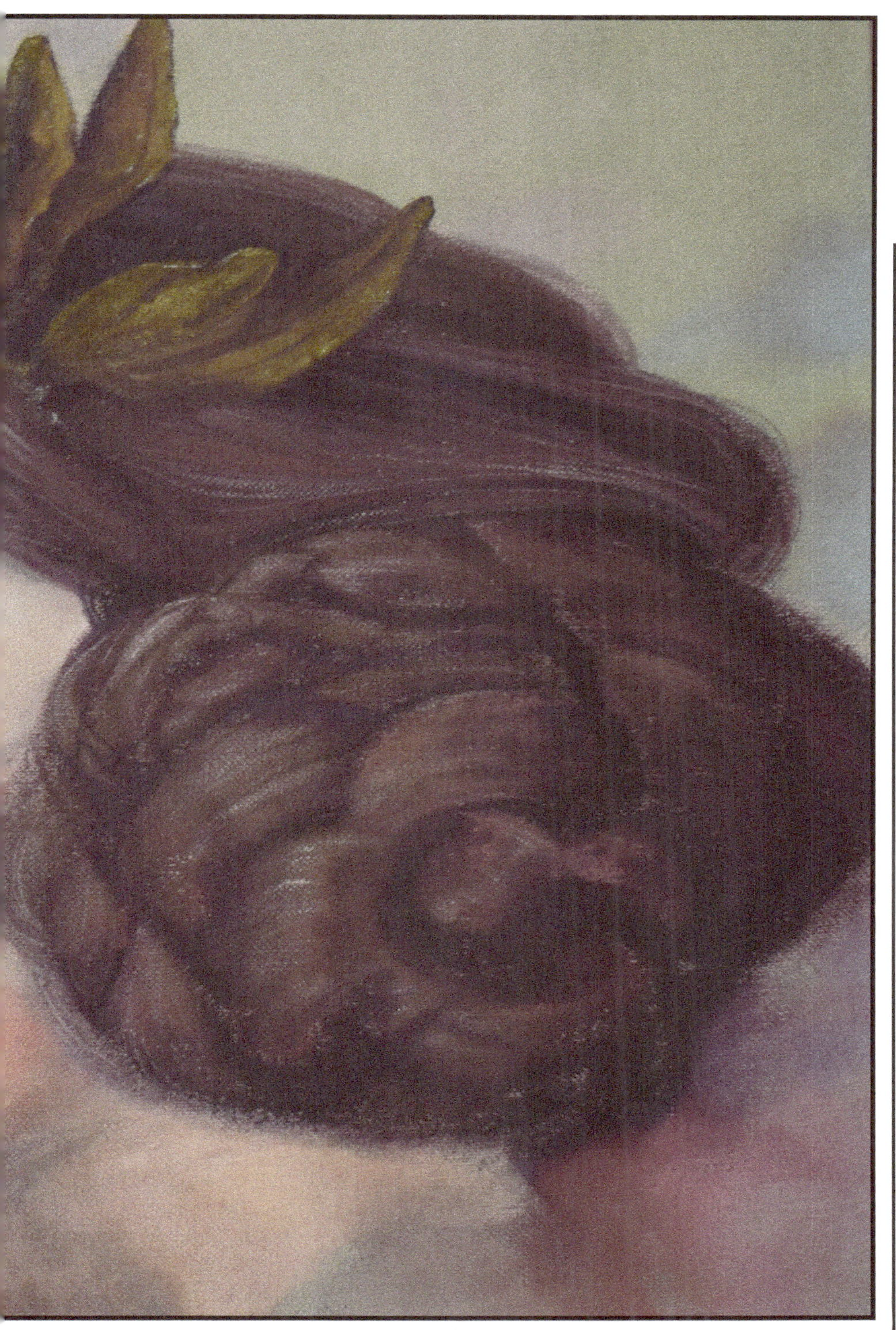

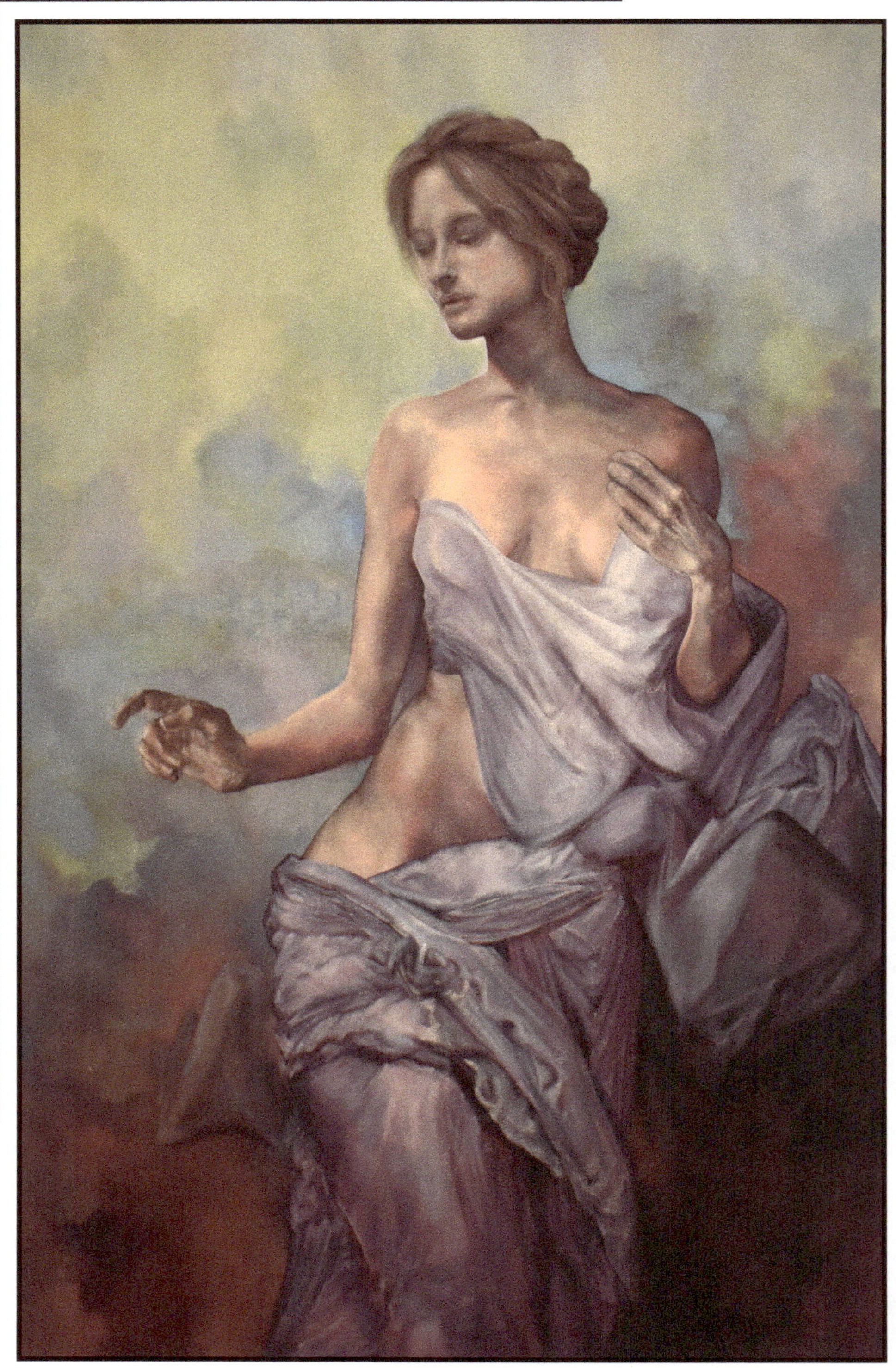

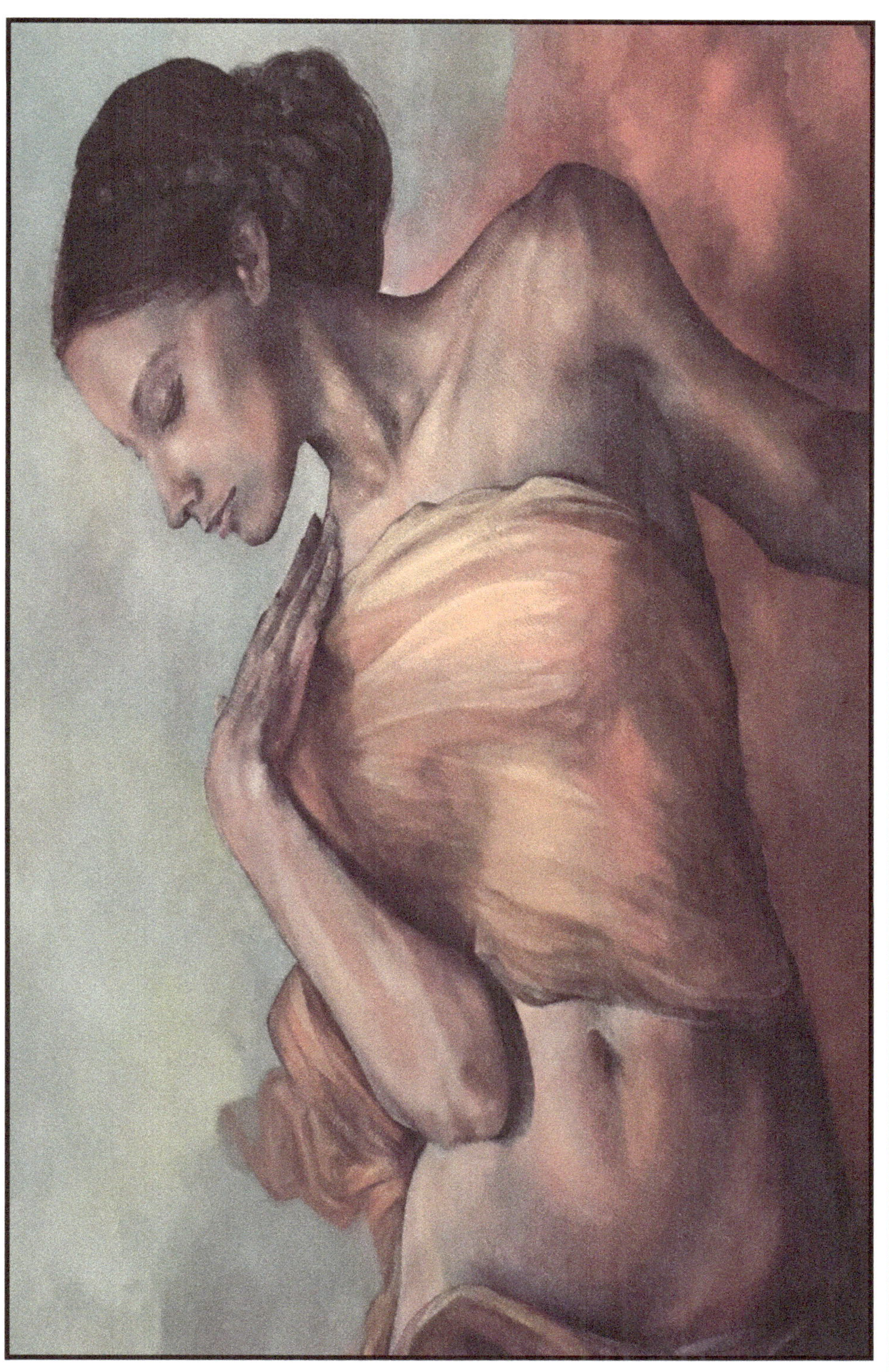

Somedays I am tired of being my father.

Cynthia Le Monds

How he took over is no mystery.

I went looking for him.

I only found things he'd left behind,

the skin he slithered out of and I have

slipped into,

like a child slipping into an old pair of shoes

with a coarse throat, splintering tongue, scarred flesh.

I had a blast pretending at first, trying out that witty tongue,

treading packed earth in worn-out soles.

Now I've lost myself in this skin; it fits me well,

a taut casing, holding the guts in—but

sometimes I can't find the words or see straight.

How little I'd known him.

The shoestring is around my throat.

I wonder how he'd feel if he knew.

Would he strip off his leather belt and beat me for getting things right

—or lean back and laugh for getting things so wrong?

Inside Writerly

Robert Eugene Rubino

Writerly is a painfully self-aware literary journal published monthly except those months in which we're told to "spring ahead" or "fall back," which we believe is an arrogant screwing around with the metaphysics of the time-space continuum.

Hardy Casterbridge (opinion, p. 2), author of the non-selling "Mixed Reviews of My Unwritten Books," is the chairman of the Palaver Prize Panel, and the founder, editor, publisher and supreme allied commander of *Writerly*.

Amanda Aintworth (fiction, p. 33) teaches The Art of Alliteration at Croftcross College of Creativity and Commerce in Covington, Connecticut. She is the author of "Hardhearted Hanna," the Palaver Prize runner-up. Her story in this issue, "Salacious Salutations," about old-boys-club misogyny in the rarified world of low-stakes literary competition, is excerpted from her new novel, "Callow Cassius," due out in either January or June or July.

Saturnina Cara-Feliz y Cara-Dolorosa (fictional memoir, p. 59) recently sold her screenplay about a female professor who, in the wake of finishing second in the voting for a rare and rarely sought-after literary prize, turns to high-end prostitution. Ms. Cara-Feliz y Cara-Dolorosa insists any similarity between her screenplay's antihero and her former colleague and partner Amanda Aintworth, or any other person, living or dead or in a cryogenically induced state of suspended animation, is purely coincidental.

Chase Roland Fetcher (nonfiction, p. 16), although born in Labrador, claims he is not now nor has he ever been a retriever. His one-man play, "Eldrick, Eldrick, Burning Bright," about the golfer Tiger Woods, was shortlisted for Way-Off Broadway's Order of Officious Offal after premiering at the Covington Cultural Centre's Pretense Plaza Playhouse, originally under the direction of his former fiancee, Amanda Aintworth, before a public falling out and bitter estrangement.

B.S. Gravitasitch (autobiographical fiction, p. 70), a co-founder of the literary agency Veni Vidi Repraesentatur, emerged as the winner of the most recent Palaver Prize, on the 51st ballot of a contentious marathon selection process finally decided by the Panel Chairman's tie-breaking vote, for "Lustful Lass, Lost." He continues to vigorously deny allegations from Amanda Aintworth that sections of his recent novel, "View From The 55-yard Line," plagiarize one of her early unpublished manuscripts. Since winning the Palaver, Mr. Gravitasitch enjoys medicating himself with codeine, valium and a tincture cocktail of THC and pure grain alcohol.

Nora Rymora-Reasoner (metafiction, p. 9) has published poetry in Latin that has been translated into 13 languages but, curiously, not yet in English, although Perversity Press, under the editorship of Amanda Aintworth, has sniffed interest. Ms. Rymora-Reasoner, former writer-in-residence at the Institute for Inner Peace on North Carolina's Outer Banks, currently lives in a trailer with her Siamese cats, Iambic and Pentameter, in Lower Intestine on Michigan's Upper Peninsula. Her story about a woman's repeated appeals to the Vatican to remove "sloth" from the list of deadly sins because "sloths are so goddamn cute" marks her debut in *Writerly*.

Macadoo Mackadont (creative nonfiction, p. 86), the celebrated parodist of Arctic Circle humor, occasionally guest lectures on the infamous 19th century polar explorer/satirist/cannibal and distant relative Ikan Ukant. He married the noted novelist, theater director and Croftcross professor Amanda Aintworth earlier this year, although it's our understanding the couple has yet to consummate the union.

Corrections. In last month's issue, what was meant to be M. Soo Laisea's retrospective interpretation of jazz icon Charlie Parker was actually an analysis of the career of basketball legend Larry Bird. Although an honest mistake, we regret the error. Also in last month's issue, Confucius Day's review of Beatrice Ooups' revisionist biography, "Satchmo: It's A Banal World," incorrectly referred to the subject's first name as Lance. It was Neil. We regret the error.

Letters. We welcome comments from readers but reserve the right to edit for elucidation, cut to the chase, paste for pastiche, distort for distortion's sake, censor obscenity and censure immorality (although we're willing to adjudicate amorality on a case-by-case basis).

Manuscripts. We encourage all writers to submit, but we cannot acknowledge receipt of manuscripts nor can we guarantee a response one way or the other before the next Mars-Venus alignment. Although we can easily afford to pay writers, we prefer not to do so. We hold as sacrosanct the venerable cliche of the starving artist.

Donations. We count on the financial generosity of our family of beloved patrons and subscribers for our continued commitment to featuring the cutting edge of literary wannabes and quasi-avant-garde ideas, although we'll take support from anyone at any time, no questions asked. Filthy lucre. We need it, we want it, you got it, you give it. Simple as a pimple.

Hooking His Thumb

Eric Forsbergh

"I look ridiculous lying here, doctor,
still inside my newly bought fishing regalia,
I, a man who lectures on Milton's Fall,
chapter, verse and line,
with all those exquisite lures
from Satan's capacious stores.
Now you and I are reasonable men.
May I sit up at least?

It hurts
this thing you call a treble hook.
Harder to remove is it?
A double-puncture?
            - so like a viper's strike -
It nailed me coming and going, yet
looking like a Walmart plastic toy.

Before I stumbled,
jerking the steel leader across this hand,
my guide – a Virgil from Cohasset –
had mentioned how carefully each lure
is designed to the temptations of the fish:
            - I said 'fish,' didn't I? –
the neon orange belly,
a dark green back with waves,
yellow flanks with spots, squiggly lines,
red reflective eyes that follow you,
a lower plastic lip to make it twitch just so,
to shimmy on a pole
            - I'm talking fish, you fool -
with ten-pound test line a lightweight sinner
couldn't break.

And now that fallen angel of a nurse,
bat wings tucked,
smile pasted on a smirk,
unwraps her gleaming implements
for surgery."

15 Times We Were All The Horse That The Cowboy Rides At The Beginning of Oklahoma!

Craig Finlay

1. When we were floating above downtown Tishomingo. We looked through the Golden Arches of the downtown McDonald's and we expected the lensing effect. Or maybe a portal. Those brick buildings will look like a Lowry painting, we said. Instead it looked like a Waterhouse. How silly did we feel? How tired we still were, too tired to care.

2. We knew I'd have to ask you "why the long face," because we were actually a horse, and we both knew we'd have to suffer that joke at some point. So the first night in Oklahoma I watched you moving from my back. You were cast in orange-speckled rain light. Then the open window and smoke. The echoing conversations of dogs and occasional dull rattle of bass in through the trunk of a hand-me down car. That was the first time you mentioned your friend Matt. How funny he was. How *talented*. How you'd known him for such a long time. I didn't think it was strange, you just now mentioning him. You never introduced me to any of your friends, they being drinkers and all. I wonder, when priests hear confession, do they ever develop the sense that this, *this is going to be a good one*, or is every sin a surprise, something to give up to the Madonna?

3. We took our guitar with us to Oklahoma. It sat in the corner for weeks before we finally tuned it and strummed out the chord progression to "In the Aeroplane Over the Sea," because no matter how long we put the guitar down we always remember it. We never got over the six-month hump of learning the guitar but we know that song don't we? Blake Shelton owns a restaurant in Tishomingo and we thought of riding into town with a guitar on our backs, like Bon Jovi. Instead it rode in the back seat of our Camry. And it only plays this one song, whether we're in the mood for it or not.

4. We let that cowboy mount us on that hillside in Nevada. His body lean and hard as an axe handle. We watched for the flash on the horizon, we watched through the glass of a welder's mask, through smoke from the camels we passed back and forth along with a bottle of warm whiskey. We talked about what horrible a thing it was, the world changing. Later, we read that they look for radiation to tell if art is fake or if expensive wine is fake, because the atomic bombs released a new element into the world—cesium 137 we learned it was

called. If something was made before 1945 — no cesium 137. How it struck us, that something so horrible is a way to shine truth upon the world.

5. We were having drinks at a bar you would miss driving by if you didn't know it was there. That kind of bar. The sign a formality. We'd only pulled off the road because you gave me head on I-80 and said you'd like something to drink now. Okay. We chased a rat terrier around some empty trailers but it wanted nothing to do with us. Chased in case it was lost, in case an owner was walking the streets calling for it, each time the fear a little more there. As recently as the 50s people used to have their pets put to sleep when they went on vacation. It was cheaper to do that and get new pets later than it was to pay for boarding. How alien, how horrifying in retrospect. Then, a few years later, we'd watch our neighbor walk her ancient, blind, toothless Jack Russell out in the common area of the duplex. She had to carry it down stairs and it shook constantly. It needed a dozen pills each day. You said humans are natural romantics, at tracted to abstract extremes. We can't just let something die at the right time.

6. Driving down here, we counted the number of insects we killed with our car. Over two days, 16 hours of driving, only three. How had we not noticed this before, that our windshields are cleaner than the windshields we remember looking through as children? We used to hit so many more insects. Splatter them across our windshields. Globally, seventy-five percent of flying insects have died off since 1990. Ninety percent of Monarchs have died. Eighty-seven percent of bees. Entomologists think most of the decline can be blamed on pesticides. They're worried because insects are the base of the food chain. Already, in France, eighty percent of partridges have vaished. When is the last time you remember a grasshopper exploding across your line of sight as you drove? Did you know that grasshoppers and locusts are the same thing? It took us thousands of years to realize that grasshoppers and locusts are the exact same species, because we decided they were a plague only when they were doing particularly well. Fewer grasshoppers means fewer plagues of locusts. No more plagues mean we can finally sin without fearing God. We all love a clean windshield. We sing about it. Oh, what a beautiful morning.

7. We rode out to Harley's Cemetery today. It's tucked in the woods and surrounded by a low stone wall that should always have at least one raven perched atop, should have it so that it seemed a kind of injustice that the wall was empty. The sign says the cemetery is

home to:

Joshua M. Harley, June 22, 1839-December 24, 1892

Nina A. Harley, March 26, 1872 - October 01, 1873

Moses J. Harley, September 29, 1876, October 17, 1877

George Daniel Cluck, March 08, 1822 - September 1822

And the four children of James Henry Neely and Nora Elizabeth Neely (nee Cluck):

Jesse Daniel Neely, January 09-1884 - October 14 1884

Three other babies (unknown names)

"How fucking goddamned tragic," you said. "There are seven children buried here and the oldest one was 18 months old."

"Life was hard on the frontier," I said.

"What a beautiful spot for a cemetery!" The Cowboy said, and began to sing.

8. We got tickets to a Flaming Lips concert in Oklahoma City. You asked if we should invite the Cowboy to the concert.

"I don't think it's his style of music," I said, "I know he's really into show tunes."

"You don't know a thing about me," the Cowboy said, walking into the room, wearing a *Yoshimi Battles the Pink Robots* t-shirt. It was the first time we'd ever heard him speak.

After the concert he sang all the way home. "Better than a magic lantern show! For fifty cents you can see a dandy show."

"That's better," you said, as he rode us down I-35.

9. I was gone for a while without telling you. I forgot my phone at home and said I was going to the gym and when you went to the gym to find me I wasn't there. You made me look you in the eye and tell you what I was really doing. When we got home you were crying and said you

thought you were done. I didn't try to argue, not even once. How easily we shed these burdens. *Buck*, horse, *buck*.

10. We went on a tour of statues. We saw The Golden Driller, the sixth-largest statue in the United States. Built for the 1966 International Petroleum Exhibition, it stands 75 feet tall. A huge golden man with one hand on an oil derrick.

"Why is he golden?" you asked.

"Because black gold?" I offered.

"But he's gold gold," you said.

"Maybe a 75-foot black man outside of Tulsa would have made some people uncomfortable," I wondered.

"Normal-sized black people in Tulsa made some people uncomfortable," you said.

"We know we belong to the land, and the land we belong to is grand!" the Cowboy sang.

So we went to Tulsa. Where Black Wall Street used to be. There's a statue there, now, called "Humiliation." A black man holds his hands up, his hat in his hand, the universal symbol of "don't shoot." We all looked very solemn, standing at the statue. The Cowboy even removed his hat.

We drove north and saw "Standing Brave," a 50-foot tall Cigar Store Indian-type statue. The kind of caricature only a Boomer could love. Feathers and a big nose and war paint. He's the first person you see driving into Oklahoma from Missouri. He guards a tax-free tobacco shop. We bought cigarettes. It was too windy to light up outside the car.

"The breeze is so busy it don't miss a tree!" The Cowboy sang.

11. When you thought I was at the gym? I went to my office to plan a picnic of artisanal pickles and salt and vinegar chips and sunflowers. This was more work than anything. An obligation. Something to signify an attentive boyfriend, like neglecting the maintenance of a highway for decades and expecting motorists to say, "My, what work they've put into the billboards."

12. Oklahoma, the same syllables as California. So simple to substitute Oklahoma for California in any of the innumerable songs about the Golden State. Oklahoma dreamin' on such a winter's day. Welcome to the Hotel Oklahoma. Adam Duritz whining that if you think you might come to Oklahoma, he thinks you should. Delta Spirit asking you to move to Oklahoma for yourself, as if they're selflessly giving you away. Tupac telling us all about that Oklahoma love. Oklahoma gurls, we're undeniable, fine fresh fierce, we got it on lock. The novelty of this wore off after a few weeks and the Cowboy just smirked in his saddle. "Yeah, go ahead," I told him, "All of the sounds of the earth are like music." He winked at me. He was always so patient.

13. The Cowboy rode alongside me as I picked up trash along Pennington Creek. You were gone. Slogging down the banks away from the campground in brand new rubber boots. The bank loam stinking. Beer cans mostly. Getting stuck. More aware of my weight when I'm sober. Wanting a drink because sometimes I break down and read Bukowski. No one will know, now. Oklahoma alone and no one will see. Digging out a can, a big gulp cup, digging out an umbrella, digging out a shopping cart I cannot take with me. Sinking into the mud and the water and my brand new rubber boots filling. The bag, torn now. Trash spilling out and floating away down Pennington Creek. I watched a new constellation form, spin, disperse, die. Digging out a tire. Failing. Chip bags and fishing lures, then shadows skim the creek. Why are there so many vultures in the skies of Tishomingo? Flocks of them. I even saw several circling the college, during the softball team's 25-3 shellacking of Paris Community College, last Thursday.

The Cowboy rolled me a cigarette in a cowboy fashion. We watched the trash float away.

"It's a scandal, it's an outrage," he said.

I spent the evening copying poems by Jack Gilbert, wondering how he can be so fucking concise.

14. We tried lecturing Oklahoma. The license plates say Native America but it's called the Sooner State, after white settlers who illegally settled the last great land grab of Indian Territory. The high school mascot is The Indians. Tishomingo is named after the Chickasaw elder who died on the Trail of Tears, is the capital of the Chickasaw nation and their mascot is the Indians. We drank and lectured Oklahoma well into the night. The Cowboy said he'd heard a lot of stories

and reckoned they were true. Tishomingo spoke in terms of a factory drone, a wailing cat in heat, the ghosts of the Harley children whispering and giggling just out of sight.

15. We were the horse the Cowboy was riding at the beginning of Oklahoma! We were in one of those two-people horse suits. I was in the back half and couldn't see anything but I could hear the corn stalks in the wind and the Cowboy singing. I said I couldn't stay bent over like this for very much longer. My back was killing me. You heard me grunting and you said we could stop. I said, "Shh! He'll hear us!" Oh my god we were so the horse at that moment.

Why I Use More Exclamation Points During The Pandemic!!

Art Bell

“Keep your exclamation points under control. You are allowed no more than two or three per 100,000 words of prose.” From Elmore Leonard’s *Ten Rules of Writing.*

Before Covid-19 came along, I was a proud adherent to Elmore Leonard’s fifth rule of writing. In my estimation, I used one exclamation point for every million words I wrote. I similarly resisted using emojis, mostly because I lacked the digital expertise needed to incorporate them into my stuff, but also because an emoji is like an exclamation point that’s gone berserk. I assume Elmore would have wanted me to avoid their use as well.

Now, thanks to Covid-19, that’s all changed!

The loneliness and isolation that’s descended during the pandemic has made the exclamation point essential to every communication. People begin emails with “Hi, Art!” indicating that if we were greeting each other in person they would be excited to see me, and I feel obligated to reciprocate.

Here’s why: How would it feel if someone waved at you furiously then ran over and jumped up and down clapping their hands before giving you a full body hug, and you stood there, emotionless, like a deer in the headlights, and gave a morose, “Oh, it’s you. Hi.” The person would be crestfallen and humiliated by the experience, and rightly so. The personal impact of responding without exclamation points is no less than a slap in the face to the other person.

For example, here’s an email I wrote recently to a friend:

Hi Mike!

I miss you! Remember when we would meet every Friday for drinks after work? I miss those tequila shots and your crazy jokes so much!! And now I don’t have them anymore!!! This Covid thing is really, really obnoxious!!!!

All best!!

Art!

To me, this is a far better way to communicate my excitement than just saying "I miss you, I miss drinking with you, and I hate Covid." It radiates warmth and affection, whereas leaving out the exclamation points indicates a lack of passion bordering on sociopathy!

So, giving the proverbial finger (!!) to Elmore Leonard's rule, I've upped my use to roughly one exclamation point every seven words.

Join me!!!!!!!!

Still not sure how to use emojis!!

Orderic in the White House

Alan Elyshevitz

Ignorant parasites, made almost mad with pride, they were astonished that such great power had come to them and imagined that they were a law unto themselves.

Orderic Vitalis, Historia Ecclesiastica

Orderic, they say, their eyes inside their skulls. *What sort of name is that?* I am an immigrant of the right kind, from a time before educated men sought history in dirt, who wrote secondhand about a javelin shower against a wall of shields. Now I need a job. I own my own hauberk, don't mind the commute. So they evaluate me with the nose-touch test and walk me through the foot-drag. Before they reveal the memos on tax cuts for sour mash and spousal abuse, they instruct me on how to transform the word "liaison" into a verb.

My first official task is to transcribe an interview with an athlete who endorses a pep drink. Every one of my colleagues is writing a tell-all for the masses. Discretely they have draped a bathrobe over the back of my chair with a brochure from Smith & Wesson in a pocket. In drawer after drawer, I uncover foiled chocolates instead of office supplies. The Resolute Desk is a docile pet that will need its teeth cleaned soon.

In the West Wing, mysterious spills appear, and slits in colonial upholstery. A clique of monastics meets in the flower shop, keeping their elbows to themselves, while many on the staff consume corked wine and ape diplomats on portable phones. On Friday a keg is delivered, which leads, it seems, to intimate contact in the Situation Room. There is bowling in the basement and tennis on a court in theshade.

Like Matilda of Flanders, the sovereign's daughter aspires to the lengthy beauty of investment. When her father is at sea, the son-in-law rules, having left prestige in his other suit. At the barricades, knights in flexible armor protect them from the tears of Gyth. The sovereign returns, withdraws to his lavatory to minister to the latest news. His senior advisors confer in conjecture. What next will the sovereign choose to occlude? He signs a decree that sullies the arbors, and another that harries unfavorable views. In this white house, he never sleeps. Tocsins call to him from tv.

Melatonin.

Sofie Rosalien Deen

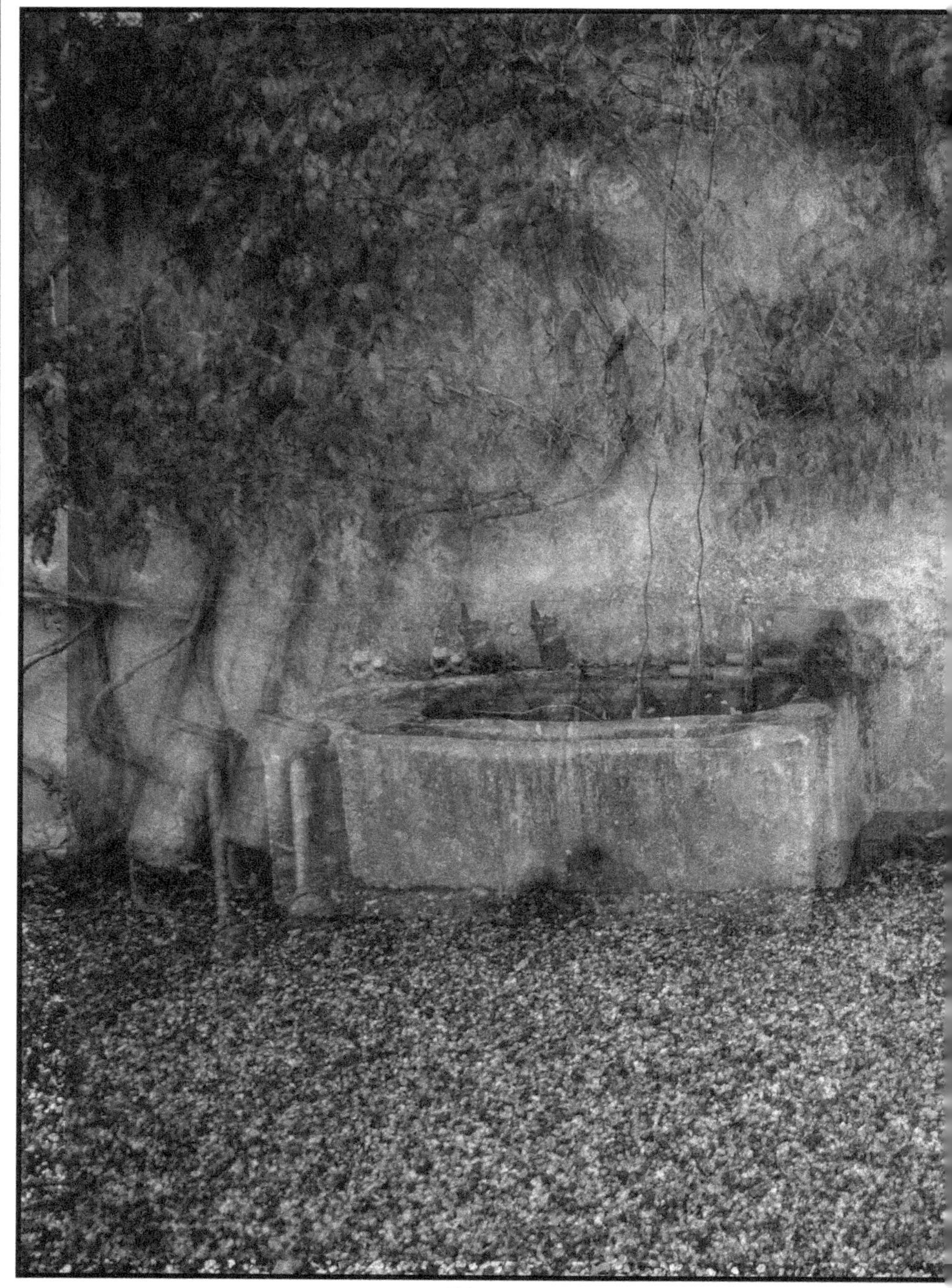

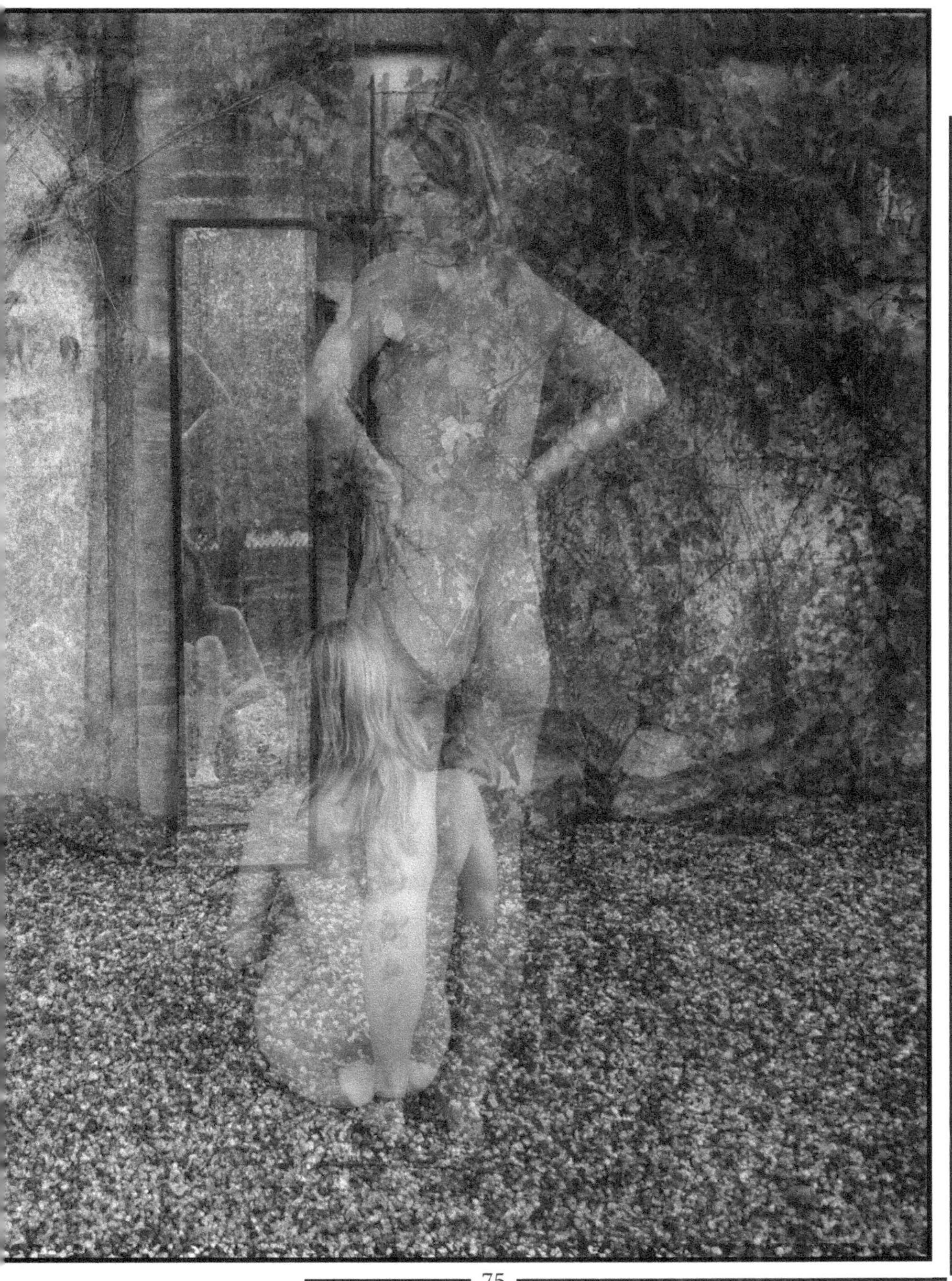

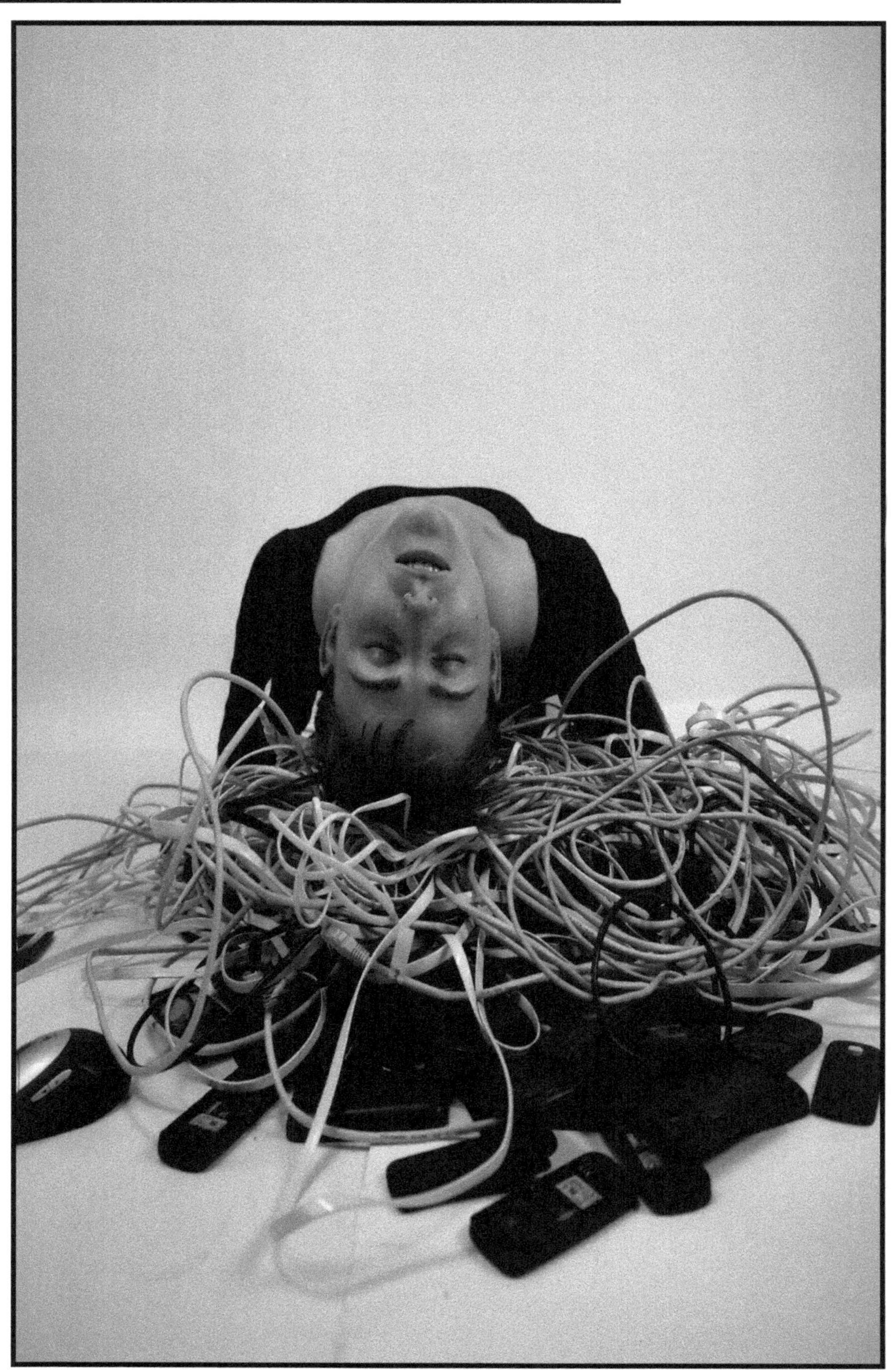

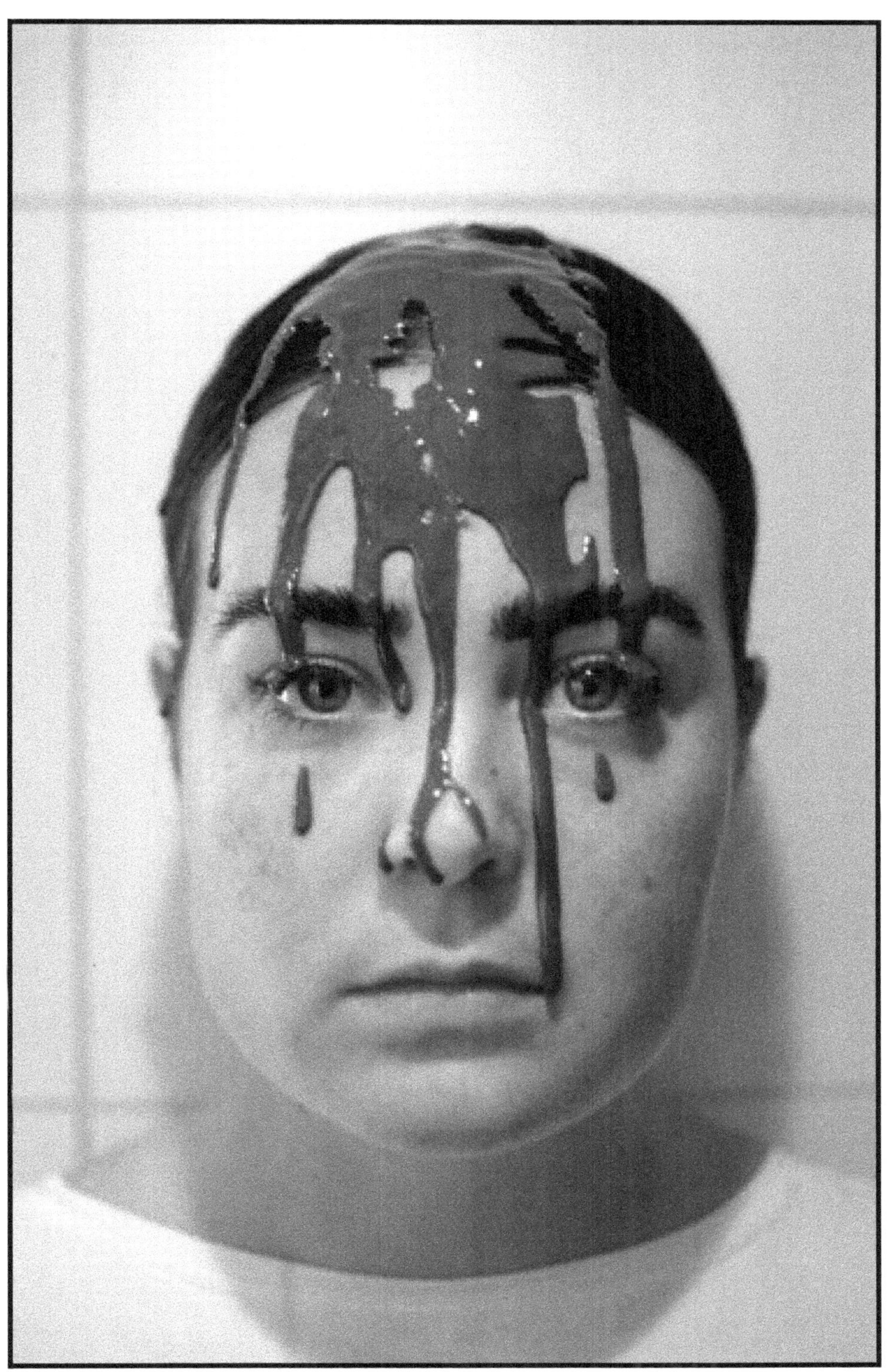

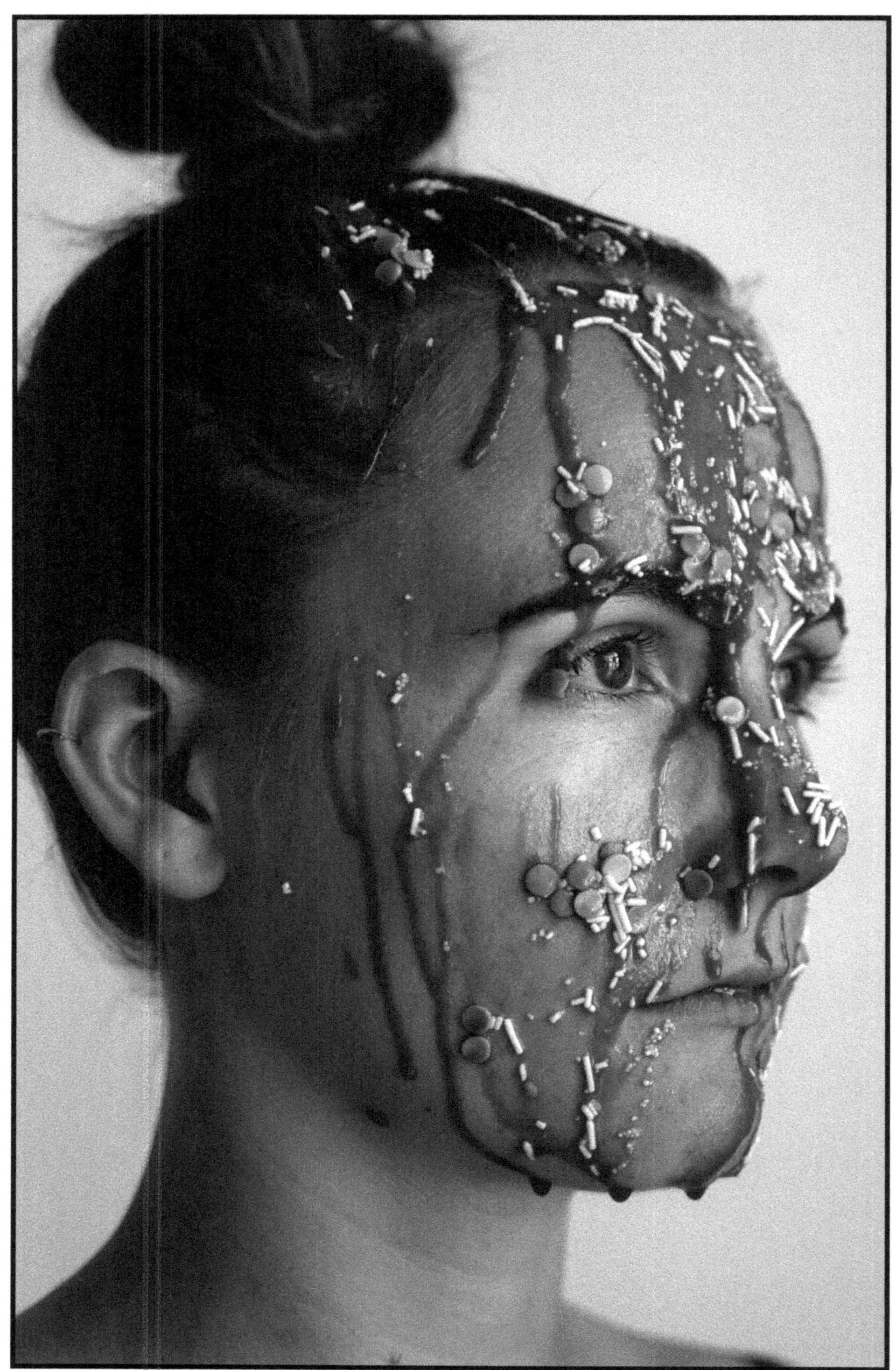

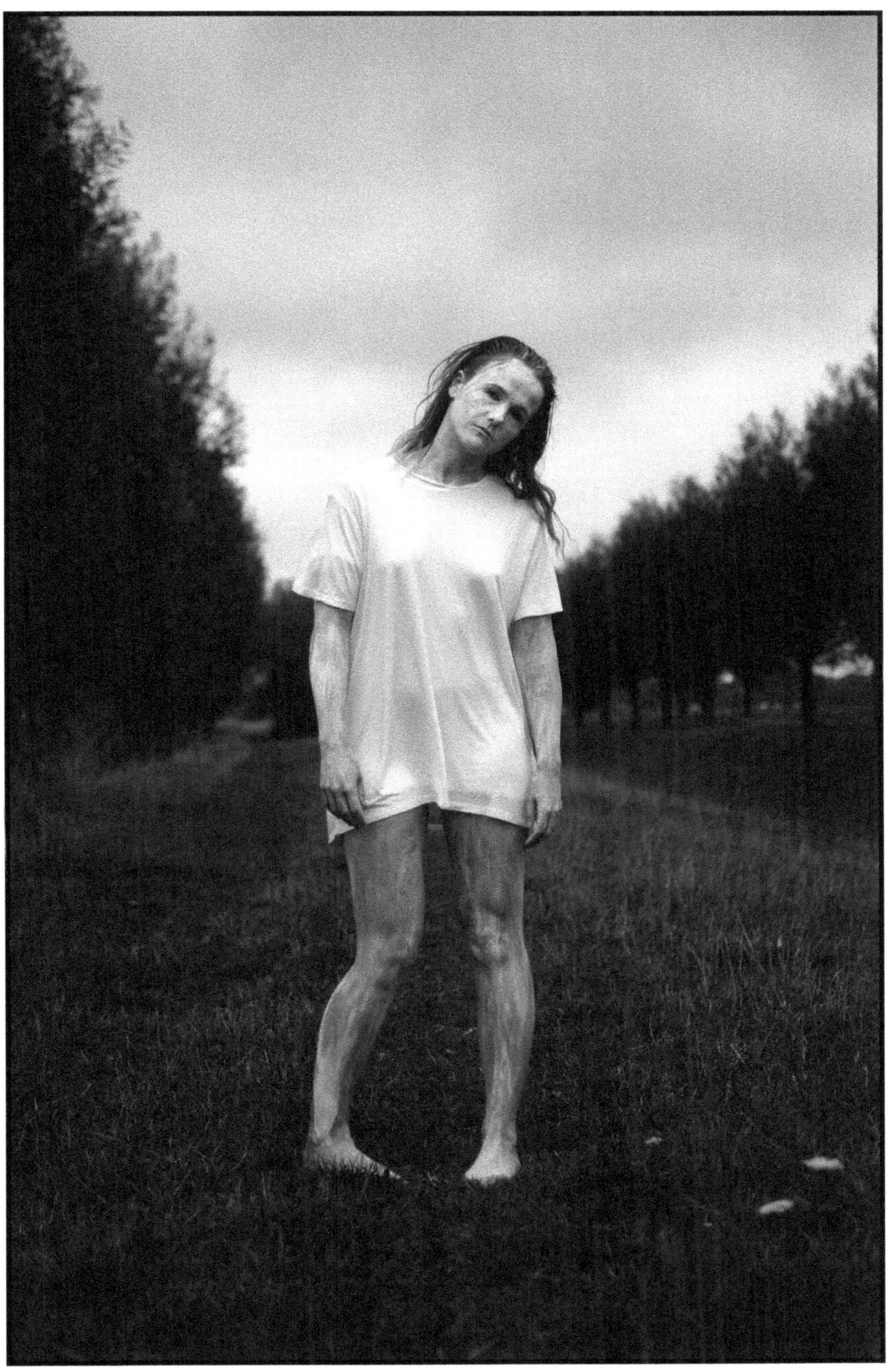

Death Mask

Art by Jack Bordnick

Poem by James Penha

If the great gods of Greece
yet punished sinners as they did
Tantalus and Sisyphus, heed here
my damnation for having failed
to speak out against the injustices
I have seen: I must witness forever
the worst wrought by mortals on
one another, one after another,
with my mouth muffled, unable
to object, to beg, to cry or scream.

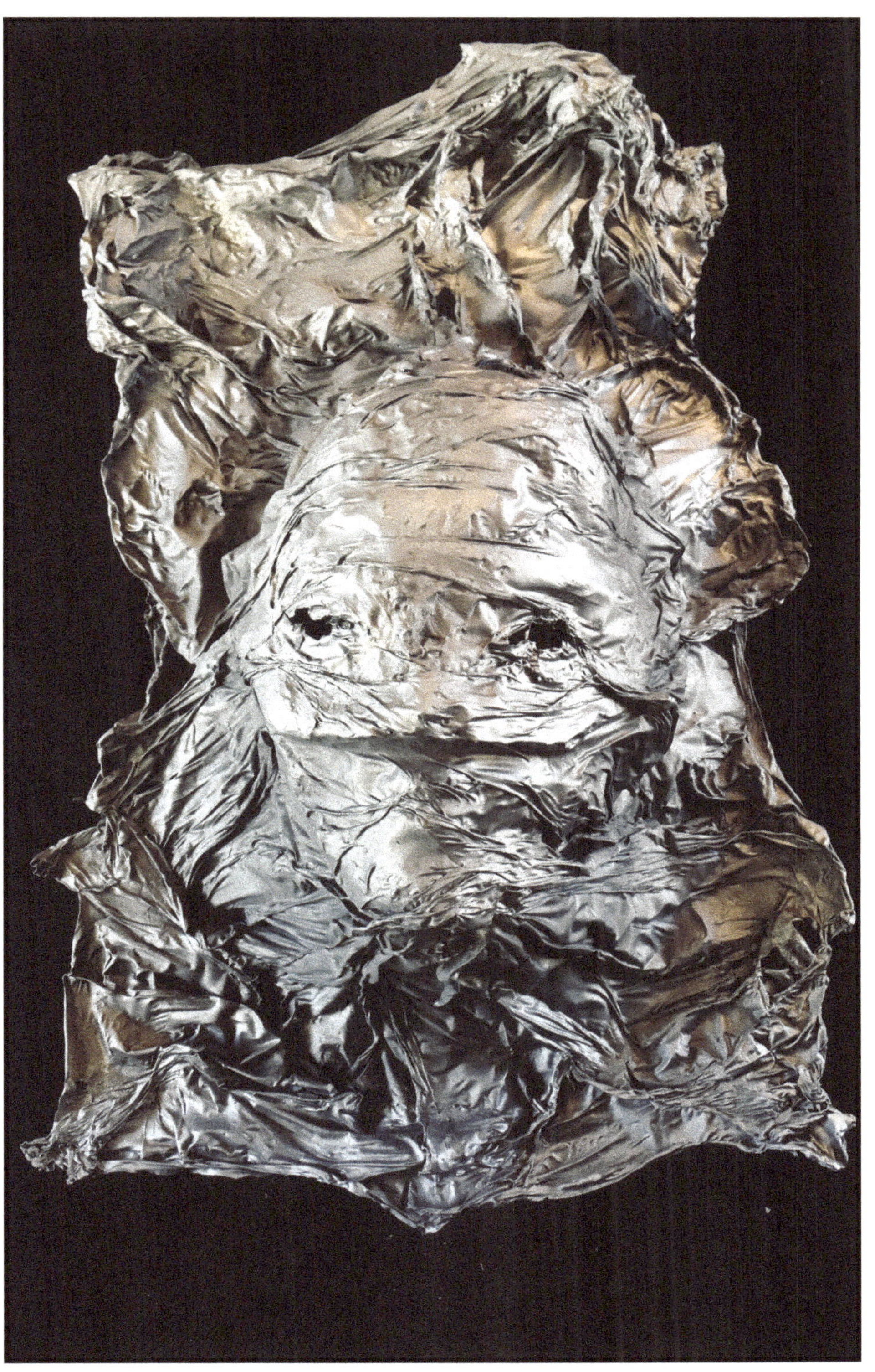

In Order Of Appearance:

Kimberly Kralowec is an attorney and poet whose work has appeared or is forthcoming in The Night Heron Barks, Birdland Journal, Star 82 Review, West Trestle Review and elsewhere. She writes a poetry blog, anapoetics.com, and lives in San Francisco with her husband and three cats. In her spare time, she volunteers as a cat socializer for the San Francisco SPCA. She holds an English degree from Pomona College and a law degree from the University of California, Davis.

J. Heimberger is a Baltimore bred nurse and aspiring poet based in NYC. Her work can be found online across several small literary journals.

Hayley Stoddard lives in Colorado, and is currently pursuing a degree in Communication. Before returning to school, she worked as a medical caregiver to disabled children and to the elderly. She began writing at a young age, and has been inspired by such writers as Billy Collins, John Keats, Emily Dickinson, William Wordsworth, Anne Lamott, Mary Oliver, and Leonard Cohen. She will be published in the upcoming issues of After the Pause, Oberon, and Beyond Words.

Mane Hovhannisyan is an Armenian fine art and conceptual photographer. The preferred topics of her art are the reflection of the state in-between magic and reality, the correspondence of the human body to the natural and urban environment, as well as the discovery of old soviet architectural leftovers through the means of photography.
She's working as a lead photographer for "Daily" newspaper of Golden Apricot International Film Festival (from 2015-2019).
Twice she was a winner of contests of Mirzoyan Photo Library "Old Yerevan" and "Landscape and Architecture", in which frames her photos were exhibited. Also honored with the "Multimedia Production Lab Grant" in Tbilisi.
In 2020 "Barren Magazine" dedicated the entire look of their issue No.17 to her photography.
Some of the images from "FABULA" cycle were published in the online magazines "Gulf Stream Magazine", "Arkana", "Wild Roof Journal", "The Closed Eye Open" and "eris & eros", also printed in "River Styx" magazine.
She had several exhibitions in Armenia and abroad. Such as the "Cyanotype" exhibition at Berlin Art Hotel and Academy of Fine Arts in Gyumri, Armenia. Exhibition "The Limb of the Sound" at Atelier Soldina in Berlin, Germany; Bunker K101, Köln, Germany etc.
She is a lead photographer of the "Quarter Tone" contemporary music organization(2016-present). Also collaborated with numerous music organizations and ensembles, including ''Artconcept', ensemble ''Assonance'', State Jazz Orchestra of Armenia, Young Artists of Opera, "Crossroads International Music Festival" with orders for posters of concerts.

Khaled K.E.M. holds a Ph.D. in Microbiology and Immunology from the University of Western Ontario, Canada. He lives in New York. He teaches biology, microbiology and genetics. He writes poetry in English, French, and Arabic. His first Arabic poetry book, El Foraq, was published in Egypt. Some of his poems written in French and English have appeared in magazines in Egypt, the US and Canada.

Caroline Weinroth is a musician, writer, and artist in Washington, DC. She earned a MFA at George Mason University. Caroline's original work has been published on NPR, Washington City Paper, and Brightest Young Things, among other places. She makes music as Cinema Hearts. Learn more at cinemahearts.com and follow on Twitter and Instagram at @cinema_hearts.

Andrée-Anne Guay was born in 1986 in Limoilou, Québec.
Her studies went from Media Arts to Archival Arts. Therefore, the fruit of her work is a pleasant combination of these two passions.
Drea's collages celebrate the beauty of the universe in all its originality and complexity. Mainly composed of archival documents, her colorful illustrations are a praise of the world's diversity.
drea.ca www.facebook.com/drea.collage https://www.instagram.com/dreacollage/

Jonathan Yungkans is a Los Angeles-based writer and photographer with an MFA from California State University, Long Beach. His work has appeared in San Pedro Poetry Review, Synkroniciti, West Texas Literary Review and other publications. His second poetry chapbook, Beneath a Glazed Shimmer, won the 2019 Clockwise Chapbook Prize and is slated for release by Tebor Bach Publishing in 2020.

K. Johnson Bowles has exhibited in more than 80 solo and group exhibitions nationally. Feature articles, essays, and reviews of her work have appeared in more than 30 publications including Sculpture, SPOT, Surface Design Journal, and The Washington Post. She is the recipient of fellowships from National Endowment for the Arts, Houston Center for Photography, the Visual Studies Workshop, and the Virginia Center for the Creative Arts. She received her MFA in photography and painting from Ohio University and BFA in painting from Boston University.

Jeremy James George is an art historian, teacher, and writer living in Chapel Hill, NC with his wife and two daughters. He is the co-author of Handbook to Life in the Ancient Inca World and has had creative writing published in Barrow Street, Seattle Review, High Plains Register, Borderlands: Texas Poetry Review, Ice-Floe, Suitcase Magazine, and Porcupine Literary Arts Magazine, among others.

Joe Pagano Jr.'s work has appeared in Narrative Magazine, Stone Shoes, Write Launch, and War, Literature, and the Arts. He was a finalist for the Wisdom-Faulkner Award and attended Columbia University.

Adam Shea Lancaster is an artist from Dallas, Texas. He creates representational paintings in a style he's called "Neo-romanti-classical"—a contemporary take on draped figures in traditional poses. His themes explore Western culture's mythical beauty, asking the important question: Is beauty as conceived by Western culture (in the Greco-Roman tradition) mythical in the sense that myth is an "untrue story" or in the sense that myth is a "storied truth."
Lancaster prides himself on creating fine art with humble craft paint from hobby shops on drop cloths from hardware stores. Although fluent in more refined media, he's made it his mission to present painting as accessible to everyone—beginning with the art students he enjoys teaching when he's not in his studio.
See more of his paintings on Instagram: @adamshealancaster.

With roots in the Mississippi Delta, Cynthia Le Monds lives in the Bay Area. She holds a BA in political science and an MPA from St. Mary's University. She's pursuing an MFA at San Francisco State University where she serves as a contributing editor of Fourteen Hills magazine. She's been published in the San Antonio Express-News and has work upcoming in Mojo | Mikrokosmos Journal, The Raw Art Review, and Kind Writers Literary Magazine. She recently placed in the 2020 Mikrokosmos Poetry Contest and is presently shortlisted for the Mirabai Poetry Prize.

Since retiring from daily journalism in 2013, Robert Eugene Rubino has published poetry and prose in various online and print literary journals, including Hippocampus, The Esthetic Apostle, The Write Launch, Haunted Waters Press, Forbidden Peak Press, Cagibi, Cathexis Northwest, High Shelf Press, Raw Art Review, MacQueen's Quinterly and Gravitas, and in the anthologies Poetic Bond IX, Earth Hymn, Poets' Choice and Poems from the Lockdown. Before the coronavirus, on most Wednesday evenings he could be found at Sacred Grounds Cafe in San Francisco, participating in the West Coast's longest-running poetry open mic. Now each week he participates online. He lives in Sebastopol, California.

Eric Forsbergh's poetry has appeared in JAMA, The Cafe Review, Artemis, Zeotrope, Ponder Review, The Journal of Neurology, Passager, Burningword Journal and several other venues. He was awarded a Pushcart Nomination by The Northern Virginia Review. He is currently a volunteer vaccinator for the local Dept of Public Health in the fight against COVID, and he is a Vietnam veteran.

Craig Finlay is a poet and librarian currently living in rural Oklahoma. His poems have appeared or will be appearing in numerous publications including, most recently, The Ilanot Review, Little Patuxent Review, Levee Magazine and After Happy Hour Review. His debut collection, The Very Small Mammoths of Wrangel Island, is forthcoming from Urban Farmhouse Press.

Art Bell is a writer and former television executive. His recent memoir, "Constant Comedy: How I Started Comedy Central and Lost My Sense of Humor" (Ulysses Press, Sept 2020), is the story of how he convinced HBO to start an all-comedy channel, and his subsequent adventures at Comedy Central during its first eight years.
Art was born in Lakewood, NJ in the mid-1950's. His father was an accountant and his mother a piano teacher. He grew up learning accounting and classical piano, among other things. In high school he co-founded and edited the satirical underground newspaper, THE TONGUE. His articles in THE TONGUE got him into trouble more than once.
After working as an Economist in Washington DC, Art pursued a career in television. He worked at CBS, HBO, Comedy Central, and Court TV.
Art currently lives with his wife in Park City, Utah where he writes, plays piano and drums, and skis.
Instagram handle: artbellauthor

Alan Elyshevitz is the author of a collection of stories, The Widows and Orphans Fund (SFA Press), and three poetry chapbooks, most recently Imaginary Planet (Cervena Barva). His poems have appeared in River Styx, Nimrod International Journal, and Water~ Stone Review, among many others. Winner of the James Hearst Poetry Prize from North American Review, he is also a two-time recipient of a fellowship in fiction writing from the Pennsylvania Council on the Arts. For further information, visit https://aelyshevitz.ink.

Sofie Rosalien Deen is a self-taught visual artist and writer with a background in Communications and Business Administration. She creates photograph series, paintings and poetry based on the subconscious. In September 2020 she created an exhibition based on her recently published poetry and photography book Raw., and is currently working on a photograph series that portray her dreams. Pieces from this serie will be exhibited in Spring 2021.
More information on her work can be found at:
www.instagram.com/sofierosalien
www.instagram.com/thegreatdanepoet
www.sofierosalien.store
www.sofierosalien.nl

Bordnick, an Industrial design graduate of Pratt Institute in New York. He have been a designer and design director for the past twenty years including for numerous company, corporate and government projects. They included a children's museum, for the city of New York and the Board of Education, involved in all aspects of marketing and design.
jackbordnickstudio.com

A native New Yorker, James Penha has lived for the three decades in Indonesia. Nominated for Pushcart Prizes in fiction and poetry, his work has lately appeared in several anthologies: Home Is Where You Queer Your Heart (Foglifter), The Impossible Beast: Queer Erotic Poems (Damaged Goods Press), The View From Olympia (Half Moon Books, UK), Queers Who Don't Quit (Queer Pack, EU), What We Talk About It When We Talk About It, (Darkhouse Books), Headcase , (Oxford UP), Lovejets (Squares and Rebels), and What Remains (Gelles-Cole). His essays have appeared in The New York Daily News and The New York Times. Penha edits The New Verse News, an online journal of current-events poetry. Twitter: @JamesPenha / No Instagram.

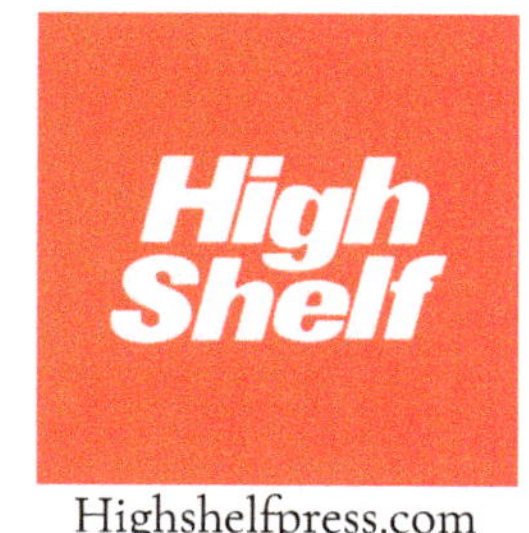

Highshelfpress.com

www.ingramcontent.com/pod-product-compliance
Lightning Source LLC
Chambersburg PA
CBHW050038040726
47599CB00015B/1731
* 9 7 8 1 9 5 2 8 6 9 3 0 3 *